For my parents, who made everything possible.

TABLE OF CONTENTS

Chapter 1
Introduction

At some level, design can be seen as a method of using creativity to impose tyranny on the world. Not tyranny in its classical sense, but rather tyranny on a much more modest, much more personal scale.

In the progression from problem to idea to solution, the designer may describe what she does in commercial terms (business requirements, technological limitations) or artistic terms (aesthetics, usability, human factors). Regardless, the most successful designs can be reduced to an essential intention: to create order out of disorder.

What kind of order? Why of course, the kind that reflects the designer's view of the world as she feels it should be. Her choices can be understood as an expression of her particular ideas of the way the world should function. It's a small, limited form of tyranny imposed on an even smaller corner of the world.

Maybe I'm projecting here. Because what I've just described is essentially an account of what first attracted me to design.

When it came to understanding "design" or "graphic design, "I entered art school at seventeen with hardly an inkling. All I knew how to do was draw with a level of competence, and my only goal was to learn how to paint for a living. But I found that when I was set free to draw and paint whatever I wanted—for that matter, when I was set loose after college as an adult—the world suddenly looked like a rather chaotic place. There was no order to it, and I knew, instinctively if not consciously, that for my particular creative skills to thrive I needed to apply them to the task of creating order, at least in my work.

I left art school without a degree in graphic design *per se,* but I spent my last year there sneaking into as many design classes as I could. In effect, I cobbled together a design education on my own, reading as much as I could and designing as much as I could for various penny ante clients, and in various design studios. I groped around for years trying to establish my particular understanding of graphic design, and formulating my own approach to practicing it. All the while I was half-aware that what I was looking for was a rigorous approach to tackling design challenges, a sturdy framework within which I could execute design ideas.

Eventually, I came to realize that in graphic design grids are the most powerful method of creating an orderly foundation for creativity. I had been trying to use them for years with mixed results, without proper training and usually without proper preparation. It's been said that graphic design amounts to little more than "lining stuff up," and for many years, that's more or less all I did. Most of my designs employed *ad hoc* grids, poorly planned columns that would arise spontaneously as I tried to "line things up." Of course, they rarely provided a stable base on which to build well-considered designs. This was especially true when I would haphazardly revise them as I went along, having almost always skipped the necessary stage of planning out the units and columns.

It took me a long time to learn how to use grids, but I learned, through trial and error, reading, poring over work from more talented designers, more reading, lots of experimentation, and finally even more reading. Grids, I came to understand, are a much deeper subject than superficial appearances suggest. I'm perpetually learning something new about them—they reward continual investigation. This, like design, like the Internet, like technology, and like the arts in general, is what fascinates me about them. Not every grid that I use or encounter is very different from what preceded it, but there's almost always something to learn from its execution.

Dots

On the very first day of a design course I took in art school, the instructor handed out blank sheets of paper to the class. He then asked each student to draw a single dot on the page, anywhere on the page.

As we made our marks, he walked around the classroom taking passing glances at where we had chosen to draw our dots, made some humorous remarks on the decisions we had made and what they suggested about our personalities. Some of us had placed them dead square in the middle of the paper, others in random parts of the page, and still others in artificially dramatic relation to the corners. Then, he asked us each to draw a second dot, again anywhere on the page. After we had done so, he told us that we had each created a design— a nearly meaningless and useless design, but a design nonetheless.

By virtue of their relation to one another on the same plane, whether spread to the far corners of the page or situated tightly side by side, the two dots we'd made suggested structure. Even in this rudimentary and skeletal form, the implication of structure was there. Indeed, the lesson was this: any time more than one element is present, there is the suggestion of a human agenda at work, a pattern of order being imposed. Design is nothing if not order applied to disorder.

Looking at the marks on my paper, I considered: if any two juxtaposed marks carry implicit structure, isn't it better to try to explicitly influence and manage that structure than to leave it to its own devices?

The immediate answer to that question came from my id. That subconscious impulse within me, seeking to find order in—or impose order on—everything, that led me to become a graphic designer in the first place. It screamed out, "Yes! Of course! Everything needs structure."

This exercise gave me a practical confirmation of something I had suspected all along: the revelation of an implicit structure in, well, *everything*. But now what I wanted from my design education was the knowledge, skills, and tools to put that order in service of solving the problems and challenges that interested me the most.

Why I wrote this book

The typographic grid is perhaps the most vivid manifestation of that
will to order in the practice of graphic design. Its structural influence
is nearly omnipresent in the best examples of the craft, as both
an expression of a designer's propensity to propagate order, and as
a practical tool to create structure for people and business.

Its continued success is based on ideas born, tested, and nurtured
in the early part of the twentieth century, when the mechanization of
communication began to change our understanding and expectations
of design.

But it's also the result of innovative and ambitious designers, artists,
and thinkers who put grids into practice throughout the last hundred
years. They turned Modernism's original, avant-garde ideas about
society, art, and technology into an enduring framework for design that
continues to dominate most of our practice and our discourse.

The historical evolution of grid thinking is something that no designer
should deny herself, but such an account is outside of the scope
of this book. The design shelf of nearly any bookstore will yield some
of the instructive and fascinating writing that already exists on grids.

However, one glaring shortcoming in this otherwise august body of
literature, and my principal motivation for writing this book, is that the
vast majority focuses on the application of the grid on paper. It largely
concerns itself with the practice of so-called "traditional graphic
design"—work whose final form results from offset printing. What's
not yet fully addressed is *how the use of the typographic grid applies
to the mechanics of digital design for the World Wide Web*. That's
why I wrote this book.

Who this book is for

This book provides object lessons in a methodology of grid-based design for creating compelling user interfaces for the Web. It will guide you through a foundational theory of how and why grids work, then take you through a series of exercises that will put those ideas into practice.

If you practice, manage, or are simply interested in Web design, this book is intended for you. You'll get the most out of it if you have a fundamental familiarity with the basic concepts of graphic design and typography and, as mentioned above, if you continue to pursue a wider design education beyond these pages.

If you're new to Web design, you'll need a reasonable level of comfort with the mechanics of website construction to really benefit from the chapters that follow. The concepts I present, and especially the practical exercises that make up the core of this book, all assume a working knowledge of how HTML and CSS combine to construct a Web page, and how JavaScript and other technologies can enhance the behavior of a Web interface. You won't need to be an expert in these skills, but you will need to understand how they work.

In fact, this book stops well short of the technical realm of implementing grids for the Web. Within these pages, you'll find no tactical advice on coding HTML, CSS, or any other technological tools, as there are any number of more qualified experts and rich resources to be found on these topics.

One final caveat

This book is not a comprehensive survey of all the thinking available on grids. It represents one particular take on the subject: my own, based on my working experience designing for digital media during the past decade and a half. That's why you won't find abstract exercises in grid theory, or solutions for every design problem you might face. Rather, what I'm presenting here is a tour of some of the design challenges I've encountered in my professional practice, with a walk-through of the techniques I employ in fashioning solutions for them.

Just as I encourage you to expand your research into graphic design and your familiarity with the technology of the Web, it's also important that you supplement what you read here with writings on grids from the pioneers and professionals who have come before me. This will give you a broader understanding of various approaches to using grids, and can only make you a smarter, more perceptive designer. In fact, I encourage you to read as much about design and technology as possible; not only grids, but also typography, layout, human-computer interaction, usability, and how design and technology are effecting change in the way we produce and consume content. (You'll find a reading list of recommended books in the appendix.) Actually, it's my hope that, whether you're new to these ideas or you're an old hand, you find *Ordering Disorder* valuable enough to earn a place on your bookshelf next to many other books on these subjects.

Chapter 2
Concept

Among experienced graphic designers working in all manner of media, the many benefits of designing with typographic grids are well known. It's worthwhile to recount the major ones here:

- Grids add order, continuity, and harmony to the presentation of information.
- Grids allow an audience to predict where to find information, which aids in the communication of that information.
- Grids make it easier to add new content in a manner consistent with the overall vision of the original presentation.
- Grids facilitate collaboration on the design of a single solution without compromising the overall vision of that solution.

These are just some of the points that you'll read in advocacy of grid-based design, but until recently they've been written primarily in the context of how grids benefit traditional graphic design. To this day, there's relatively little writing about the grid as it applies to digital media and user interfaces, a fact that I find puzzling.

After all, a graphical presentation on a computer monitor is already rendered through a de facto grid system of very fine proportions: a monitor display is composed of seventy-two tiny pixels per inch, arranged vertically and horizontally like an incredibly tight sheet of graph paper—a grid, in fact. What's more, this is a grid authored by mathematics.

In the predigital world, the most intricate and flexible grids were developed with a degree of mathematical precision; grids gained acceptance because their usage reflected the mathematical harmony found in nature. In online media, rather than merely using math to draw a grid with a ruling pen, grids are actually constructed directly from math. Every line, box, typographic specimen, or image that appears in a digital grid is directly produced by mathematical calculations made by the computer.

So we can think of this machine-level grid in the same light as the structure created when two dots are placed on a blank page: it's implicit and ever-present. There's really no such thing as designing without a grid in digital media, because at least at a very basic level, to design anything on a computer is to design within its mathematically generated grid of pixels.

It follows, then, that Web designers—those who have a predisposition to order—would want to exert an explicit influence on and management of the elements they're putting on a computer screen, to accept that reality and harness its power. The grid seems like a natural fit.

In fact, revisiting the benefits listed, we can understand quickly that they all apply easily to designing for the Web:

- Grids add order, continuity, and harmony to the presentation of information on frequently high-density web pages.
- Grids help users predict where to find information from page to page or from behavioral state to behavioral state, which aids in the communication of that information.
- Grids make it easier to add new content to a website in a manner consistent with the overall vision of the original website.
- Grids facilitate collaboration on the design of a single website without compromising the overall vision of that website.

In some ways, these benefits seem more salient on the World Wide Web, where structure and order are prized perhaps even more than in print media. Though the primary tool for accessing information on the Internet is called a browser, the predominant pattern is that users search for information and accomplish specific tasks—not so much browsing as seeking. This is behavior for which grids are ideally suited; grids help Web users find things and help Web designers place things where they can be found.

Whether a designer works in print, on the Web, or in some other media, it's my belief that the biggest benefit grids provide is that they are excellent facilitators for creativity.

For those with only a passing familiarity with what it means to work with grids, this assertion might seem counterintuitive. Many novices assume that grids are by appearance—and therefore by nature—confining, that they restrict freedom of expression and stifle creative impulses.

Though this idea was once persistent even among many experienced designers, time has proven it to be false. In his essential 1978 book *The Grid,* Allen Hurlburt prefaced an otherwise *tour de force* exploration of grid ideas with this somewhat defensive opening statement:

"At the outset, it should be pointed out that this book is not an unqualified recommendation of the grid as a primary force in graphic design. Many highly qualified contemporary graphic artists—even in Switzerland and Germany where grid systems originated—are producing outstanding work without the use of formal grids."

More than three decades later, this kind of cautionary approach
to grid design seems anachronistic. Experienced designers have by and
large accepted that grids are an aid to the practice of our craft, with
few caveats. In 2009, the noted designer, author, and design thinker
Ellen Lupton said:

"To say a grid is limiting is to say that language is limiting,
or typography is limiting."

We can think of grids, therefore, as a springboard for creativity.
They lay a foundation through which a designer can create solutions
to problems large and small, and in doing so help readers, users, and
audiences find that which all humans seek: a sense of order within
the disorder.

Invisible order

Of course, we all look for different kinds of order, or we look for order in our own particular ways. Designers, in particular, may not seek the same kind of order that less visually-trained people might. By profession, we have taught ourselves to detect visual or programmatic patterns: Do things align? Do they conform to similar shapes, scales, or patterns? Do they employ similar visual formatting? Are they sorted by some kind of schema? Is there consistency even among things not immediately visible? This is what we're doing when we're evaluating any design, when we're viewing a web page, or when we're mentally tracking our experience as we click through a website.

Most people, though, tend to look for order less critically, at least in the visual realm. They look for a *sense* of order, and not necessarily for the *fact* of order. They ask themselves consciously, or more often subconsciously: Do things feel as if they're in order? Do they follow some fundamental rules of logic? In fact, you might say that what people seek is *the absence of disorder* as much as the presence of order.

The intricacies of any given ordering system may be lost on most people, but the presence of that ordering system can nonetheless be felt. So a user of an interactive system—a website, a kiosk, or a mobile application is unlikely to explicitly understand the overarching design principles at work in that system, at least not immediately. On the other hand, a user of an interactive system can *sense* that the features of that system—its content, its tools, its navigation— are constructed according some overarching design. If he encounters some evidence that there is order in place, his confidence in and sense of ease with the system increases dramatically. An ordering system need not announce itself, and it may never be consciously understood, but its presence is nevertheless significant.

This is not to say that a sense of order can be merely superficially fashioned, as many designers try to do by creating grids that are not thoroughly constructed. An ordering system cannot be easily faked; a designer cannot convincingly impart the feeling of an ordering system without order actually being present. The more exposure the user has to that system and the deeper she digs into its features, the more important it becomes that the ordering system be a thoroughly organized one. Its logical tenets must hold up and bear out under the scrutiny of actual use. It doesn't matter that many users may have only a superficial sense of the ordering system; they will not reap the benefits unless the system has been thoroughly and well designed.

Grids, of course, are a type of visual ordering system. Like ordering systems of any kind, they work on these two levels: first perception, then experience. That is, a user feels the grid, then he uses it.

A brief history

Let's step back for a moment. Designers correctly trace the origins of the grid concepts with which they're most familiar—the typographic grid—to the early part of the last century. That was when a handful of architects, printers, typographers, and designers effectively reimagined the graphic arts as a reflection of universal principles rooted in nature, mathematics, and the rise of mechanization. This is an accurate reading of history (to which we'll return shortly), but also an incomplete one. It can be argued that since time immemorial, everything mankind has perceived has been subject to our continual search for order. Man being man, our search is less a quest than a process of creation. Where there was no order, we created it.

In her amazing history of the grid as a conceptual framework, *The Grid Book,* art historian Hannah B. Higgins writes :

"In the Babylonian creation myth, God turned men out like bricks from clay molds. It was men who built bricks into walls. The first grid, the brick wall, easily evokes associations with the human body."

Tracing the origins of the brick back as far as 9000 BCE, Higgins argues that the very first of these building blocks was indeed a reflection of man. They were of a size that could be both shaped by hand and, in the absence of machinery, could be moved by hand. Though they were man-made, and therefore imperfectly shaped, the design of the brick was sufficiently uniform that *any* man could make a brick. He could be confident that the end product would still fit the original vision, and would contribute to the bigger goal of raising a wall. Once compiled into those walls, the bricks formed a grid—a visual grid of rational consistency—that was also a method for understanding the world. For a brick wall is quite literally a way of imposing order on the world, of physically organizing one's environment by separating what belongs outside from what belongs inside. This logic was so natural and so compelling to man that it persists undiminished to this very day. With great ease, it was extrapolated across geography: bricks formed walls to organize the immediate environment, walls defined parcels of land, and these in turn formed cities. Today, countless people live, work, and play within this simple conceptual framework; the urban grid that methodically or organically gives form to metropolises everywhere is a powerful organizing principle of everyday life.

Mathematical formulae

Bricks are simple to create, use, and understand, but more sophisticated thinking on ordering systems has also evolved over the centuries, and these discoveries and innovations have informed our thinking on grids. By turning to math, to nature, and even to our own bodies, we have sought to unlock hidden logic and order in the world throughout the ages.

In the sixth century BCE, the Greek philosopher Pythagoras posited what came to be known as the Pythagorean theorem, a mathematical construct that describes the three sides of a right triangle. This theorem became a conceptual building block of geometry that every math student learns, often without truly understanding why. More importantly it shows that the relationships between simple numbers suggest an innate order, and indeed Pythagoras's legacy marks the elevation of mathematics to a philosophical framework for understanding the world.

Pythagoras is also credited with being the first to recognize the golden ratio, which describes harmony between two numbers of a specific relationship (approximately 1:1.618). Often called the golden section, its nuances are complex and challenging, providing countless hours of fascination to some of the greatest mathematical minds in history. The golden section has also been a source of inspiration to artists and architects since the Renaissance or earlier. Those who have used it in constructing buildings or allowed it to guide the composition of paintings have found it to be of unparalleled value in producing aesthetically pleasing works—some of the most historically significant masterpieces the world has seen.

The Fibonacci spiral reveals a grid that man has found useful for centuries.

Appropriately, the golden ratio is intimately tied to another captivating mathematical concept: the Fibonacci sequence. Introduced to Western mathematics in the thirteenth century by an Italian mathematician, it has been traced back as far as 200 BCE in ancient India, where it was employed in the sciences.

The Fibonacci sequence commonly begins with 0, then 1. Each succeeding number is equal to the sum of the two numbers that precede it, so the first several numbers in the sequence are:

0, 1, 1, 2, 3, 5, 8, 13, 21, 34, 55, and so forth

Any number in the Fibonacci sequence, when divided by the number that immediately precedes it, yields a quotient very close to the golden ratio number of 1.618, sometimes lower, sometimes higher. As the numbers increase, the quotient converges progressively closer and closer to 1.618. What's more interesting to designers is that the Fibonacci sequence, when expressed as a logarithmic spiral, forms the basis for a grid that is instantly recognizable as harmonious and logical.

The ISO 216 paper standard, used around the world, is based on the √2 rectangle.

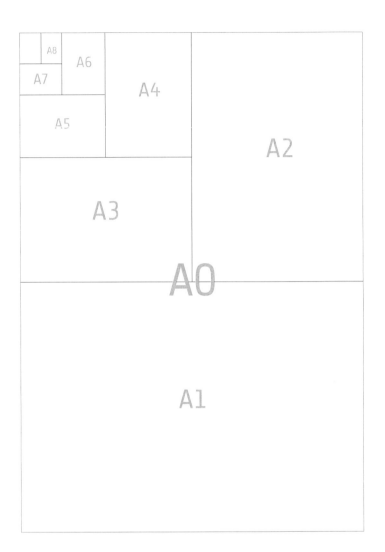

A very similar grid can be formed from a $\sqrt{2}$ ("root-2") rectangle, which is occasionally confused with the golden rectangle. $\sqrt{2}$ rectangles, when divided in half, retain the same ratio of width-to-height that the original rectangle possessed. This is of particular note to designers, as these rectangles are at the core of the international standards for paper sizes (ISO 216, based on the German DIN 476 standard). Though not employed in mainstream American commerce, this paper standard successfully spread across Europe and to many other nations in the twentieth century. It was even adopted by the United Nations as an official document format. More to the point, it was a uniform approach to the manufacture, distribution, and use of paper. This had a profound impact on the work of graphic designers in countries where it was adopted, as it facilitated their designs and provided a standard against which they might choose to work.

Less scientific is the so-called rule of thirds, which is in fact not quite a rule and only superficially mathematical. Dating to the eighteenth century or earlier, it provides a rule of thumb that painters, draftsmen, photographers, and graphic designers (but few architects) have applied to the problem of achieving aesthetically harmonious compositions. It contends that compositional strength can be found by dividing any image into three columns of equal width and three rows of equal height. The intersection of the dividing lines forms four focal points to which the human eye is naturally attracted. The rule of thirds holds that by aligning elements with the dividing lines or placing elements at these focal points, a maximum of interest, energy, or tension can be communicated.

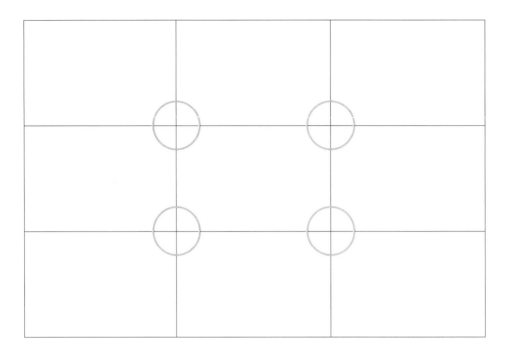

The rule of thirds identifies four focal points within most any composition where the human eye is naturally attracted.

Perhaps as a result of its lack of intricacy, the rule of thirds is perhaps the most obviously useful of these various "formulas" for aesthetic desirability. Its simplicity is persuasive, and the technique of straightforward, equal-thirds division is easy to remember. This is particularly instructive for us in considering the more mathematically sophisticated methods discussed above. The contributions of the golden ratio, the Fibonacci sequence, and other mathematical innovations to the long history of grid understanding is undisputed, but for most routine situations, their usefulness is limited by their inherent complexity.

Thankfully, the golden ratio, the most valuable of these for designers' purposes, need not be studied at a master level to be useful. The exercises later in this book will include a practical approach to its day-to-day use. The key lesson for now is that the more straightforward the method employed to build a grid, the more effectively that grid will be built.

The twentieth century

These and many more strands of theory came to inform major changes in the design of communications in the twentieth century, graphic design's pivotal epoch. Its first two decades carried forth the legacies of what might be considered the premodern design world. Graphic works were executed largely through tradition or intuition, with emphasis placed on imitating the natural world or emulating historical but often poorly understood models of aesthetic ornamentation.

The 1920s and 1930s brought a revolutionary shift toward a rationality that directly addressed new, mechanized media. The early proponents of this so-called Modernist approach to design included El Lissitzky, Kurt Schwitters, Jan Tschichold, Paul Renner, László Moholy-Nagy, and others, most of whom practiced in Germany and many of whom taught at the famous Bauhaus school. They insisted on a new paradigm for ordering the world: form followed function, systemic thinking became an imperative, and standardization was prized. They rejected the rote emulation of natural forms and embraced instead the inherent beauty of the industrial machines that were then remaking society.

The rise of fascism in those same decades displaced many of these practitioners and their ideas, as the Bauhaus shut its doors in 1932 under the brutal hand of the Nazis. Many relocated to Switzerland, where there existed a strong affinity for their ideas, and their approach to graphic design continued to flourish. The International style, as it became known, cross-pollinated Bauhaus ideals with a complementary tradition of rigorously applied simplicity and minimalism. Central to this, of course, was the notion of grid-based design, of tapping into the inherent structure of every page to create a sense of order in every design. Under the expert hands of Swiss designers like Josef Müller-Brockmann, grids informed nearly every design decision, geometric forms became more and more emphatic, and the mathematical underpinnings of every element became less and less hidden. The Swiss style, as it is sometimes known, quickly catalyzed into a highly refined visual vocabulary that many regard as an artistic peak for graphic design.

Meanwhile, many former key Bauhaus figures had immigrated to America, where their ideas took root in the country's postwar boom. From the late 1950s on, these designers worked alongside design émigrés from other European countries and leading American counterparts like Paul Rand. They helped to develop the Modernist framework for order into an aesthetic ideal and an essential component of twentieth century commerce that suffused American life. Modernist graphic design—and the grid—transformed the country's visual landscape in a few decades, and it remains integral to our visual vocabulary even today.

The Internet

Graphic design, as perfected by the scores of practitioners who labored over it in the twentieth century, gave us a profoundly rich foundation for written and pictorial storytelling and organization. Its theories and practices are critical to our understanding of how people consume and act on information. When the commercial Internet dawned in the 1990s, that body of knowledge helped to form a basis for how we would envision the World Wide Web, too: as a series of pages, each composed of the same building blocks as a printed page—titles, subtitles, paragraphs—to be presented, read, and consumed in much the same manner.

As a conceptual framework to help transition a mass audience from print to the Internet, graphic design proved invaluable. It helped the Web to recreate much of the visual vocabulary of analog commerce, fostering a sense of familiarity in the intimidating expanse of online space. Both long-standing and startup brands tapped into the inherent power of graphic design, and used its principles to bring about the breakneck expansion the Web has seen over the past twenty years.

Before too long however, the limits of strict adherence to a graphic design-centric approach to the Internet became obvious. Analog design challenges, while complex and rewarding, had always presented problems of a fixed nature that required solutions of a fixed state. A book or a magazine, or even an identity system, requires a designer to create a single, canonical design. That design may need to evolve over time, to change with different circumstances or editions, but in each expression—a single edition of a book, a single issue of a magazine, a single business card or letterhead—the solution appears and functions in the same way for everyone who encounters it.

Not so on the Web, where a design solution may have an infinite (or at least inordinate) number of expressions based on the hardware or software being used to access it, or even the explicit or implicit preferences of the user. Where print asks, "What is the solution?" digital media asks, "What is the solution—and how does it change based on the various circumstances under which the solution might be accessed?" The content of a given web page may appear radically different from one person to the next based on each user's profile, for instance. Similarly, the typography of the page may appear bigger or smaller owing to the browser being used to view it.

Indeed, the technology being used to view a given piece of content on the Web can be nearly as important a factor as the content itself. Analog design solutions rarely required any technological aids to be consumed, yet in digital design, certain technological specifications are prerequisites for every solution. There is no Web design without a Web browser, to put it bluntly, or a computer of some sort, for that matter. What's more, all browsers are not built equally, nor are the computers on which they run uniform in their capabilities. So the tools that people choose or have access to can produce very different renderings of the solution.

For these reasons, then, the principles underlying typographic grids are significantly different on the Web:

- A grid solution on the Web is critically dependent on the technology available to the user for its successful rendering.
- Typography is, at least for the time being, fundamentally unstable online, varying greatly from user to user, and potentially frustrating the ability to produce desired results with the grid.
- There is no canonical size for a Web browser, both because the physical size of users' monitors will vary, and because the user may actually have her browser window reduced or expanded beyond its default size. As a result, the grid lacks the same luxury of a fixed, knowable sheet size found on the printed page.
- User inputs, preferences, and settings—which can be made both passively and actively—can drastically alter the requirements for an online grid solution.
- While precision placement of elements is possible on the Web, the grid is limited to increments of pixels, and pixels themselves vary in scale from device to device.

Given the highly variable nature of Web design, we can begin to think of print design being relatively definitive in nature. Analog design solutions are declarative, whereas Web design solutions are conversational. A solution for a Web design problem embodies a kind of conversation among the designer's intention, the technology at hand, and the user. What's more, communication on the Web (and in all digital channels) is increasingly concerned with facilitating conversations among users, creating frameworks within which highly unpredictable kinds of content can flow back and forth between people. It's useful to think of Web design as being similar but fundamentally different from what came before it in the analog world.

How different? To answer this, it helps to think of these two modes as everyday communications: the declarative tradition as a speech given before an audience, and the conversational mode as, well, a conversation between friends or acquaintances.

A speaker invited to address a crowd may not be able to predict perfectly how well her talk will go over, but she still has a good idea of the conditions under which she'll deliver it: at a podium, on a stage, with the audience sitting facing her, saving their questions until the end. By contrast, a conversation might begin with a clear agenda and a proactive participant may help to guide the discussion, but conversations are nearly always as unpredictable as they are predictable, if not more so.

Similarly, the experiences that audiences take away from a speech are generally uniform; every audience member has his or her own opinion of how well a lecturer might have done behind the podium, of course, but the entire audience heard the same talk and sat in the same room, making for a compelling commonality. With a conversation, however, experiences can be wildly divergent. All of us can recall walking away from a conversation with an understanding of what was said or agreed upon that was dramatically different from—or even contradictory to—what other conversants experienced.

Indeed, speeches are intended to be received by their audiences; a speaker talks *to* those who sit before her, not *with*. The size of the audience hardly matters either; a speech prepared for a hundred people is hardly different from one prepared for two hundred. By contrast, a conversation is a shared experience; to participate in the conversation is to become one of its collaborative authors, and probably to alter its course as well. And if there are no participants, there is literally no conversation.

A shift in communication

In the context of the relatively short history of the Internet, this shift from declarative to conversational communication feels sudden and novel, an abrupt course correction that rewrites the rules. But there is some historical precedent for what we're experiencing. We can view it as a kind of long-running tension, in which the modes are both complementary and concurrent, with one or the other dominating during given periods throughout human history.

In his 2007 book, *Glut: Mastering Information Through the Ages*, designer Alex Wright discusses the origin of writing as an early form of bookkeeping, a method to record simple contractual agreements that previously had been sealed only through verbal confirmation between two people. In this way, the objective nature of writing served as a counterpoint to the far more subjective nature of human conversations. Writing, in effect, made laws and governments possible, and so came to dominate over the less defined, more argumentative nature of simple conversations.

Similarly, at the point when various civilizations collapsed, and faith in government and in laws dwindled, the power of conversation was resurgent. In the wake of the Roman Empire's demise, for example, a tradition of folklore emerged that held sway over groups of dispossessed people.

In the absence of mass-produced books or more sophisticated media, folklore was a kind of conversation between storytellers and their audiences, communicating basic ideas through repetition, memory, and word of mouth.

When Johannes Gutenberg invented movable type printing presses in the fifteenth century, the pendulum swung back toward declarative communication. Through mass-produced printed matter, ideas, facts, and narratives could travel great distances without diminishing the authority of the original text. The printing press undercut the persuasiveness of storytelling and conversation, and established a new framework for understanding the world: if it was in print, it must be true (or at least it stood a better chance of being true than something overheard).

This push and pull even repeats itself within the relatively brief history of the digital age. When computing hardware began to propagate in the second half of the twentieth century, it was largely a declarative medium. Mainframe computers were confined to tightly held laboratories and managed under strict conditions; only designated users could access the machinery, and then only for specific tasks and for strictly managed durations. With the advent of the personal computer, computing escaped into the wild, so to speak, becoming available virtually anywhere, at any time, and to anyone—it became a conversational medium. And it's that same conversational nature of computing that has effected such profound change on graphic design in the form of the Internet.

What's even more critical about this history is the idea that in none of these instances did one mode supplant the other: the advent of writing and contracts hardly did away with handshake agreements, it merely complemented them. In fact, if anything, it built on the tradition of verbal agreements. Folklore in many ways carried forward the ideas of the Roman Empire, the spirit of its laws and government, if not the letter of them. The printing press found great success through reprinting those same folktales. The personal computer continued for many years to tap into the power of mainframes through vast networks, and the idea of strictly guarded computing servers has hardly gone away.

When we use the grid for the Web, we must be responsive to our users, we must create experiences around the fact that they will not just consume them but *use* them, too, and so we must take into account the grid's behavioral dimensions as much as its formal dimensions. We must also keep in mind that the grid is not a tool to impose order on users or to usurp their control; it is a tool to impart order to our users, so that they can create their own experiences.

So why was this digression into the study of communication and history important to learning about grids? For the simple reason that having the larger context of the problems we're solving is useful in creating better solutions for them.

By drawing a distinction between these two modes, we can understand that the design problems they present are fundamentally different. At the same time, if we understand that there is a long-running push and pull between these two modes of communication, that in many ways they are complementary, then we can see that they can borrow from one another as well.

Conversational design has borrowed significantly from the foundation laid by twentieth-century print designers. At the same time, it has combined it with equally significant borrowings from the worlds of human-computer interaction study, computer science, and product design, among other disciplines. The result shares striking similarities with the declarative tradition, but at the same time this new mode is something very different.

The typographic grid was a tool originally designed to solve declarative design problems, but in this context it is also a legitimate and useful tool for solving conversational design problems. The caveat, for those who practice its use and for readers of this book, is that in using it we are also obligated to adapt its principles to the new constraints of the Web. As designers, our charge is always to design for the problem at hand, not to emulate problem-solving techniques that came before. The truer the solution is to the medium we're designing for, the more apt it is.

Chapter 3
Process

The balance of this book focuses on how to build a grid, including an overview of the steps to a working solution. Before we begin, though, it's useful to outline principles that every designer should keep in mind.

A grid should focus on problem solving first and aesthetics second. A grid can provide such a seductive aesthetic enhancement to any design that it's tempting to focus on its beauty rather than its utility. Many designers become preoccupied with the beauty of the grid and contort content or functionality to squeeze it in, regardless of how uncomfortable or ill-suited it may be. But the most successful grids are built in service of well-defined problems. Whether they're communication problems, organizational problems, or transactional problems, a grid derives its beauty from how well its resolves those challenges.

A grid is a component of the user experience. A grid is not a tool to impose complete control over a user's experience of a website. Rather, a grid is a framework within which the user can control his own experiences. Designers should not force every element and interaction to occur within the grid, nor should they allow the user experience to be unformed and unpredictable. It's the designer's job to make certain decisions for the user—not every decision, but enough so the user can accomplish his goals unhindered. The grid is a tool for that job.

The simpler the grid, the more effective it is. The principles described in this book can be used to create grids made up of sixteen, twenty, or even more units, in any combination of columns of uniform or irregular width. However, the fact of the matter is that the designer should always strive to create the simplest grid possible. As we'll see, mathematic precision is a key element of good grid design, but mathematical *usefulness* is just as important. The formulas you use to calculate combined units and columns should be fairly straightforward, even simple enough to do in your head or to explain quickly to a colleague. The simpler a grid system is to use and to explain to others, the more users will benefit from that grid system.

Steps

Here, then, are the major steps in designing a grid solution:

1. Research and requirements
2. Wireframes
3. Preparatory design
   - Pencil sketches
   - Units, columns, baseline development and calculations
   - Page sketches
4. Comps
5. Production (code)

Keep in mind that though our thinking should be rigorous, our process need not be. Though the order in which I've presented these steps has been useful to me, it may not necessarily work for every designer. Not every step must be followed in exactly the same order, for a specific amount of time, in a specific way, or even at all. For example, step 3, preparatory design, is a set of three different activities that are often done concurrently, with the designer switching between pencil and paper, software, and back-of-the-envelope math as necessary. What matters is not the rote repetition of these steps, but following the principles of good grid design throughout.

All the same, it's worth spending some time up front to discuss two critical steps in this process. The first is research, and the second is sketching.

Research and constraints

We first judge truly good design not by its beauty or its innovativeness or its efficiency, but rather by how well it responds to its original problem. Successful solutions demand that the designer grasp the problem presented to her and the constraints within which she's working. The designer has to ask and understand the answer to questions such as: *who* is the audience, *what* is the context, *when* will the solution be encountered, *how* will the solution be used—and even *why* is the solution necessary?

These questions can be difficult to answer, and the answers themselves are often unclear or difficult to parse. A designer must be persistent in asking them, in pressing for good and accurate answers, and in thoroughly examining and comprehending those answers.

Because a grid can give us such a head start in creating solutions, it can be tempting to forgo this stage of the process. Once a designer masters the rudiments of grids, it becomes much easier to start the mechanical process of constructing units and columns than to do the hard work of asking and answering these questions.

But nearly every design problem demands a period of thoughtful study before the search for a solution begins. Without a clear sense of the challenge at hand, any design work—including the development of the grid—is done in vain. It's a much more productive use of time to do research at the beginning of a project than to jump straight to the design.

Grid-based designs are no different. The more completely the problem is investigated, the better the grid will be. Well-researched grids maximize the creative options available to the designer. They also anticipate and avoid the traps of prematurely constructed grids: inappropriately structured units and columns, grids that are good for some aspects of the problem but inadequate for others, grids that fail to account for constraints that may not be obvious at the outset, grids that prove so unworkable that they need to be rebuilt at inappropriate times, and grids that prove unusable for collaborators.

What kind of constraints should the designer look for? They fall into three main categories:

- **Technical constraints** determine the delivery of the design solution. They include the target screen resolution and the generation or "modernity" of the target Web browser, two critical factors for any design. Often, technical constraints regarding a site's publishing system are important elements as well; the designer needs to consider limitations that such systems might impose on how the content is output. A publishing system frequently affects how content creators produce content for publishing, the workflow, which in turn influences the kind of design solution that can be put into place.

- **Business constraints** determine the very purpose of the solution. Whether it's to increase visitor traffic, time spent on a site, click-through performance to advertisements, or conversions of site visitors to customers, these goals are the most important imperatives for any design solution. The designer should consider branding, positioning, and marketing considerations as well. Finally, she should fully assess the business's ability to maintain the solution she creates: who will need to work with the grid after it's completed, and what are their skills.

- **Content and editorial constraints** determine the production of the content. They account for the different forms content might take, such as the types of articles, their length and the length of their headlines and summaries, pull-quotes, images and embedded content such as video and interactive elements, data tables and charts, and so forth.

Of course, designers will bemoan the inconvenience of constraints, or perhaps the thorniness of some of the particular constraints they must contend with. If only those constraints were lifted, if only the problem were slightly different, then the solution would be much easier to arrive at or more elegant in nature.

However, these constraints have a silver lining: in some ways they might make a problem more difficult, but they can also make it easier to arrive at a design. Comprehensive solutions like grids can often benefit from being built around one or two nonnegotiable constraints, immovable requirements that can't be easily altered during the design process. To begin with, they can directly influence the proportions of a grid, the very sizes of the units, columns, and regions that the designer constructs. These kinds of constraints might appear to limit the options available to a designer, they very often also have the effect of increasing a designer's inventiveness. The more wide open a design problem and the less restrictive the constraints, the less a designer is likely to make those insightful leaps of logic that are the hallmark of great design. Nonnegotiable constraints can help spur a designer to do this. Whether it's locking in a particular dimension, a technological imperative, an advertising unit, or some other factor that a designer must work around rather than conveniently modify to her own needs—having one immovable requirement can be enormously useful.

Sketching

Having spent so many paragraphs belaboring the importance of thoroughly researching a problem, I can make this next point more succinctly: sketching on paper is an essential tool for thorough design problem solving, and it's particularly helpful in developing grids. The simple act of quickly and loosely drawing out speculative combinations of columns and potential layouts can save vast amounts of time and often leads to much more creatively fertile grid solutions than simply jumping ahead to designing or even coding a grid.

I can't emphasize enough the power and usefulness of using old-fashioned pencil and paper to work out problems, to brainstorm potential solutions, and to explore promising or even not-so-promising ideas that may be too costly or time consuming to test otherwise. In fact, the most important aspect of sketching is not so much making marks on paper, but rather being able to run through many ideas quickly, with little cost. Remember, you have no expectation that the sketches will amount to anything more than just sketches. Sketches don't need to be pretty.

As mentioned earlier, it's also important to keep in mind that sketching need not be a discrete phase of constructing a grid that begins and ends at specific points. Sketching can happen at any phase throughout the project, at multiple levels of completion—though of course it's most useful to sketch earlier, so that more ideas and possibilities can be run through very quickly. Keeping a pencil and a pad of paper handy at all times is sure to prove invaluable.

Terminology

The vocabulary that describes the various components of a grid might seem simple, but it can also be surprisingly unspecific. For example: the notion of a column seems straightforward enough, but on a page based on an eight-column grid, a designer might create a layout with only two columns of text, rendering the meaning of that term imprecise. Even books about the craft of grid-based design don't always agree on terminology, with some using terms (e.g., regions, fields) that are missing from others. For the purposes of this book, then, it's important to establish some common ground terminology as we proceed further into more practical discussions of grids.

UNITS

The building block of any grid, a unit is the smallest vertical division of the page (i.e., units are measured in width), upon which columns are built. Units are typically too narrow to house most textual content.

COLUMNS

Columns are groups of units, combined together to create workable areas for the presentation of content. Most text columns, for example, require two or more units to be workable. A grid system of, say, sixteen units can be combined into two columns of eight units each, or four columns of four units each, and so on.

REGIONS

Regions are groupings of similar columns that form parts of the page. For example, in a four-column grid, the first three columns from the left might make up a single region for the display of one kind of content, and the remaining column might form another region.

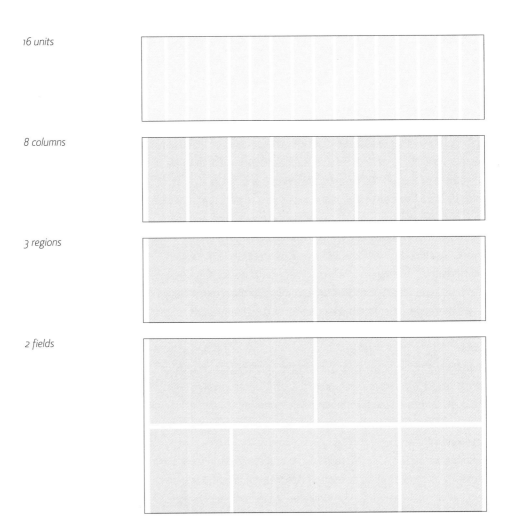

16 units

8 columns

3 regions

2 fields

FIELDS

Fields are horizontal divisions of the page (i.e., fields are measured in height) that help a designer to visually pace the placement of elements on the Y-axis. Fields can be calculated in many ways, but using the golden ratio is one of the most effective methods.

Lorem ipsum dolor sit amet,
consectetur adipiscing elit.
Curabitur scelerisque odio
vitae lectus tincidunt porta
pellentesque urna placerat.

The baseline grid is based on the invisible lines on which letterforms rest.

BASELINE GRID

In traditional typography, the baseline is the invisible line on which letterforms rest, e.g., the bottom edge of a capital *E* rests on the baseline, while the descender of a lowercase *p* will fall below the baseline. The baseline grid is formed by a uniform, top-to-bottom repetition of baselines spaced apart according to the leading or line-spacing of the text.

HORIZONTAL VS. VERTICAL ORIENTATIONS

These concepts are notoriously easy to confuse (a unit can be thought of as either a horizontal or vertical division of a page, depending on one's point of vew), so this book refers instead to the columnar grid (divisions of the page measured in width) and the baseline grid and regions (divisions of the page measured in height).

GUTTERS

Gutters are the empty spaces between units and columns. When units are combined into columns, they incorporate the gutters between them, but not the space to the left of the leftmost unit nor the space to the right of the rightmost unit.

MARGINS AND PADDING

Margins are the space outside a unit or column. Padding is the space within a unit or column. Margins are generally used to create gutters, while padding is generally used to create a small, visible inset within a block of text inside a column.

ELEMENTS

An element is any single component of a layout. Examples include a headline, a block of text, a photo, or a button.

MODULES

Modules are groups of elements, combined to form discrete blocks of content or functionality. A registration form, for example, is a module composed of several constituent elements such as a label, a form field, a button, and so forth.

Chapter 4
Execution

There's no better way to learn how to design with a grid than to actually roll up your sleeves and try it. Now is the time to put all that theory, history, and preparatory study to work. This section focuses on creating a practical solution to the challenge of designing a website.

There is, of course, no such thing as a typical website or even a typical Web design problem. But the job we'll focus on in this section combines many common types of pages, including a blog, profile pages, and a home page that knits together disparate content types. The project also illustrates many different design challenges that will be instructive in showcasing a general approach to real-world grid design. Taking all of the project's constraints into account, we'll construct a single grid system and apply it to the various page types found throughout the site.

A side note: this section, and indeed this book, were written and designed so that readers can start reading anywhere, and I fully expect that many will buy this book exclusively so that they can skip ahead to this very section. There's nothing wrong with that, of course. Still, it's worth mentioning that, just as the ideas and context provided in the preceding chapters are of limited use without the practical advice that follows here, it's also true that the how-to instruction in this section will be of limited use without the ideas that precede it. The next 120 or so pages will provide you with the tools, but the preceding chapters are meant to provide you with the creative skills necessary to make good use of these tools. Don't cheat yourself!

The job at hand is to design an online design journal—a website by, for, and about designers. It will combine editorial content in the form of blog publishing and a social networking layer into a cohesive user experience.

The site is composed of four major templates. We'll take an in-depth look at how to construct a grid that works for all of them, then apply that grid to the design of each. As we work through each template, the various constraints and lessons will build on one another:

- Blog article page
- Category/catalog page
- Profile page
- Home/gateway page

Later in the book, we'll extend that solution across a number of secondary templates, which will help demonstrate the flexibility of our system. These include:

- Messaging pages (e.g., error pages)
- Blog index pages
- Preferences pages
- Calendar display pages
- Email templates

Since we're dealing in the hypothetical, we'll also assume a make-believe name for our design journal: Designery.us. This gives us some grounding in the branding requirements for our project, which we'll discuss in greater detail soon.

Getting started

UNDERSTANDING THE REQUIREMENTS

If there's one lesson you should take away from this book, it's that understanding a project's constraints is the first and most critical step in crafting a solution. We must identify the criteria that determine whether the outcome we create will be successful, or even workable Until that is accomplished, there's little point in thinking about the grid we might develop, much less in unpacking our digital design tools to start choosing typefaces and colors.

For Designery.us, we will suppose the preexistence of a set of well-documented wireframes prepared by an information architect. Wireframes are schematic drawings that capture the features and types of content that are required for each template. These wireframes do much of the job for us; in fact they function as documentation of many (though not all) of the constraints that inform the project.

At this point, we won't account for the constraints presented by every template throughout the site. Instead, we'll focus on the four major templates that will form the basis of the majority of pages. If we design our solution thoughtfully, we trust that whatever grid we develop can be easily applied or adapted to the less critical templates later on.

In reviewing the wireframes for those four main templates, we can identify two principle constraints. These, helpfully, are fairly clear cut and reasonably typical of many Web design challenges: the viewport size and the advertising unit.

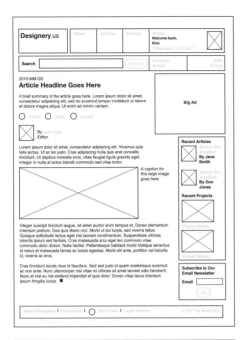

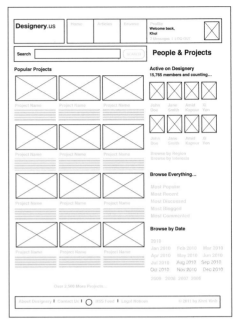

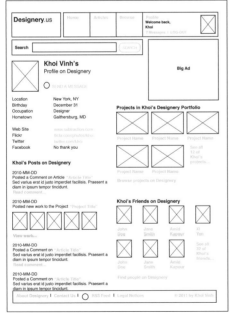

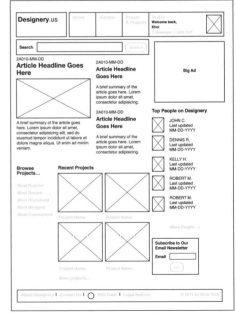

THE VIEWPORT

It seems unlikely that we'll ever have a single, standard size that all Web browsers will adhere to. Even as desktop screens get ever larger, our attention will continue to be divided among the much smaller screens on our mobile devices, the medium-sized screens that are becoming common with tablet computing devices, or the large-scale screens on our high-definition televisions. (Paradoxically designers must treat large television screens like lower-resolution devices because users sit far away from them.)

However, as this book goes to press, at a still early juncture in the Web's development, it seems reasonable to say that 1024 pixels wide by 768 pixels tall is as close as we come to a canonical size. Or, rather, it's the most utilitarian of the handful of standard screen resolutions we can work within. It's neither too small for most reasonably sized displays nor too large for the increasing power and resolution of handheld devices.

So the first constraint is that our design must fit into a 1024 x 768 screen.

Of course, a 1024 x 768 screen doesn't translate directly into a viewport of that same size for a web page. Thanks to menu bars, the tendency of most browsers to be sized slightly smaller than the space available to them, and other bits of user interface overhead, most browsers have a natural "posture" about 20 percent smaller than the total screen real estate. Within that browser window, we'll also want to accommodate some minor padding on the left and right sides of the window, so our design doesn't abut either edge, reducing the available viewport even more.

A 1024 x 768 screen is as close as we have to a standard screen resolution. This will serve as one of the constraints for our design.

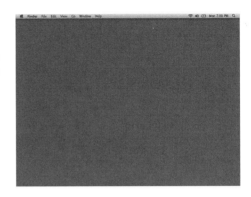

A browser's natural posture inside a screen makes roughly 80 percent of the screen available to users for viewing any web page. This makes for a space within the browser of about 974 x 650 pixels.

Assuming some visual padding on the left and right edges of the browser, this reduces the available screen real estate—or "live area" to approximately 960 x 650 pixels.

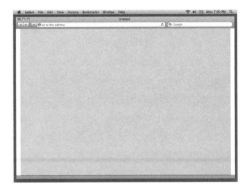

THE ADVERTISING UNIT

Looking at our wireframes, we see right away one shared requirement: a rectangular ad unit is a prominent feature. It may not appear on every page, but we can recognize immediately that whatever grid we construct needs to work with this ad unit. This ensures consistency across the site.

For many Web designers, ads are the bane of our craft. They present a particularly touchy kind of constraint that often seems antithetical to creating well-designed user experiences. By their nature, ads are intended to disrupt the flow of the user experience that designers try to orchestrate in our solutions.

The rather obvious fact of the matter, however, is that for many sites, advertising units are their very lifeblood; they provide the revenue that allows the sites to run. In spite of their inconvenient nature, they're a very real and important constraint.

That also happens to make them a very useful constraint, too. We have discussed the paradox that the less mutable the constraint, the better the design problem. A prominent advertising unit is helpful to us in that it provides a foundation on which to build our grid; it effectively informs the way the grid is shaped.

For our purposes, we'll use the Internet Advertising Bureau's "big ad" unit, which is 336 pixels wide by 280 pixels tall, as our second constraint. As it happens, the width of this particular unit specification can also accommodate at least two other sizes of ads: the 300 x 250 medium rectangle unit and the 300 x 600 half-page unit. That is, a design created around the big ad unit should be fairly easy to use for these other ad sizes.

A THIRD CONSTRAINT: THE BRAND

The viewport and the advertising unit are our two most critical constraints, but it would be irresponsible to proceed without acknowledging an equally important factor: the brand. While the influence of the brand on the construction of a grid-based solution is less direct than other constraints, it's nevertheless an important factor in the overall design solution. The grid you build for a youth brand, for instance, might be less restrictive than the one you might build for a financial services brand.

For the purposes of this exercise, we'll make some straightforward assumptions about the Designery.us brand:

- The audience is designers of all ages and Internet experience levels.
- The overall tone should be friendly, well-organized, simple, and uncluttered.
- The logo should be prominently displayed.

SUMMARY

Having run through these criteria, we now have enough information to define the problem at hand. Before moving on to developing the grid itself, it can be useful to summarize these constraints to prevent any possible miscommunication. This is best done by restating the problem in a simple, concise paragraph:

Design the basic site templates for an online design journal. The site combines blog articles and social networking layers into a cohesive package, as outlined in the wireframes on page 50. The templates should accommodate a minimum screen resolution of 1024 x 768 pixels with a live area of approximately 960 x 650. The structure of the page must accommodate an IAB standard 336 x 280 ad unit. The completed design should reflect the Designery.us brand's design-savvy, uncluttered tone; feature its logo prominently; and use its red, black, and white color palette.

The designs for each of the pages in our site begin with hand-drawn sketches.

Sketching the solution

As with every design problem, the best path to a solution starts with sketching. Using pencil and paper, we can run quickly through several different approaches for a design framework that will work across the site. Again, the focus is on the four main templates, and in fact we only need to create sketches for those pages, but it can be helpful to keep the secondary templates in mind during this process as well.

In sketching, the goal is not to create a drawing of a completed solution, but rather to think as creatively as possible through approximation. Sketches should be fast, loose, and small in scale—a single sheet of paper is more than enough room for at least a half a dozen sketches done in quick succession. It's not important at this point to sketch an exact grid or to determine the number of units in the solution. Instead, focus on the number of columns to be used on a given page, regardless of how complex or difficult it will be to create those columns mathematically. In sketching, we want to remain as free as possible to come up with creative solutions, and let those ideas in turn determine the grid we'll construct later.

After several rounds of this visual brainstorming, we'll settle on these rough sketches to guide us as we begin to construct the grid.

Notice that these sketches take considerable license from the preliminary layout suggested by the wireframes: the name of the site is pushed to the far right and occupies a larger proportion of the page, some of the navigation items have been changed or consolidated, and there is a much different balance between the elements on the page and white space. As designers, this sort of interpretation is part of our responsibility. It's not enough to simply translate the wireframes—we must also *interpret* them so that the final outcome is the best, most coherent user experience we can design. If some cases call for looser interpretations than others, it's also the designer's responsibility to engage the other stakeholders in discussion over the departures from the wireframes that designers feel are necessary. In short, for designers, the creative process has its origins here in the sketching stage.

It's also worth repeating that sketching need not be an isolated part of the process. It's important to keep a pencil and paper handy even beyond this initial sketching phase, in case we need to return to sketching to work out previously unforeseen problems. This ability to sort through many creative possibilities in short order can be invaluable throughout the design process.

CONSTRUCTING THE GRID

ESTABLISHING THE COLUMNAR GRID (UNITS)

In print, designers base the sizes of units and columns on the fixed constraint of the sheet size they're working with. The final size of the printed page, poster, or panel directly influences the mathematics of the grid. In Web design, though, the closest equivalent to a sheet of paper—the browser window—is volatile, if not unreliable. This is where having a fixed constraint as described in chapter 3 is enormously helpful; in the problem at hand, the advertising unit is preordained and therefore serves as a handy ballast for the design as a whole. Again, everything flows from our constraints.

To translate the rough columnar structures implied in our sketches into an actual, mathematically precise grid, we can apply any of the many readily available Web-based tools that will create solutions in an instant—but I'm going to employ a trial-and-error method that will progressively reveal the critical decision-making that produces a comprehensive solution.

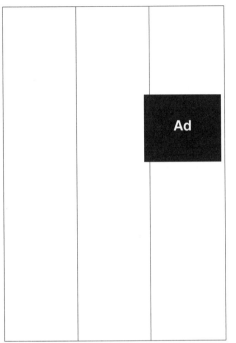

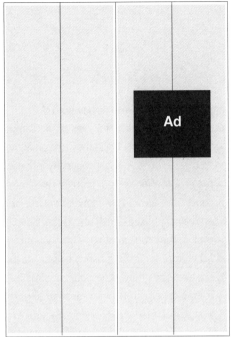

Dividing the page into
three equal columns
doesn't work
with our ad unit.

And neither would four
equal units, which
would require too wide
a column for the ad.

First we'll start by making simple, clean divisions to the page. Our sketches imply a two-thirds/one-third column structure, in which the left region is twice as large as the right region. Remembering that our viewport is 960 pixels wide, we can divide the page into three columns of 320 pixels each.

This would be an elegant basis for our grid, but of course this column size would be insufficient to house our ad unit of 336 pixels wide. It's possible to reduce the size of the left region and increase the size of the right region, but if we do that we wouldn't be creating a rational grid but rather an improvised one, and we'd be sure to encounter problems later. The goal here is to create a *uniform* set of divisions of the page that will give us layout guidance across the range of design problems we will encounter in this project.

Assuming that we'd add at least five pixels of margin to the left and right sides of that ad unit to prevent it from bumping up against the column edges, we know that our right-most region would need to be at least 346 pixels wide. Multiply that by three and we find that such a grid would already require 1,038 pixels in width, which exceeds the maximum width of our viewport significantly—and that isn't even taking into account additional width necessary for column gutters. As helpfully simple as a straight three-column structure would be, this problem calls for some more subtle calculations.

The next logical option is to divide the page into four units of 240 pixels wide each. That lets us combine the two rightmost units into a single column of 480 pixels, which will obviously give us plenty of room for our ad, but more room than we really need. What's more, it renders the two leftmost units too narrow to function as columns; the two-thirds/one-third balance of the design would be gone.

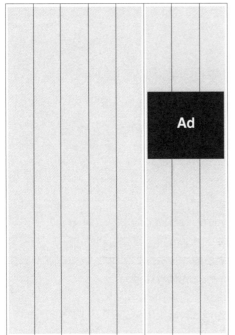

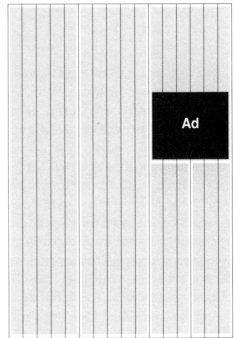

Units and columns in multiples of four often point to the right solution. Here the page is divided into eight units.

To let us create a more fine-grained set of columns, we'll subdivide those eight units into sixteen.

On the other hand, units and columns in multiples of four very often point to the right solution, even if they're not workable in and of themselves. (Indeed, most sound grid solutions are made up of four, eight, or sixteen columns, so it's often useful to create new grids with that in mind.) If we divide the page into eight units of 120 pixels wide each, that allows us to combine three of those units into a 360-pixel wide column, which can comfortably accommodate the ad unit. That would leave a 600-pixel-wide left region, which restores the original two-thirds/one-third balance we're seeking, and will function well as the main text region on our article page. However, this left region would be composed of five units, an awkward number should we need to create further subdivisions.

The improvised answer to this problem would be to simply divide the left region into two columns of 300 pixels wide each. In effect that's what we'll do, but we can use this opportunity to make a more thoughtful decision. By subdividing the grid even further, from eight units of 120 pixels wide each to sixteen units of 60 pixels wide each, it allows us to create a more fine-grained set of columns. The left region can be divided into two columns of five units each, and the right region can work as a single column of six units or, if it needs to subdivided, two columns of three units each.

*Our final
sixteen-unit grid.*

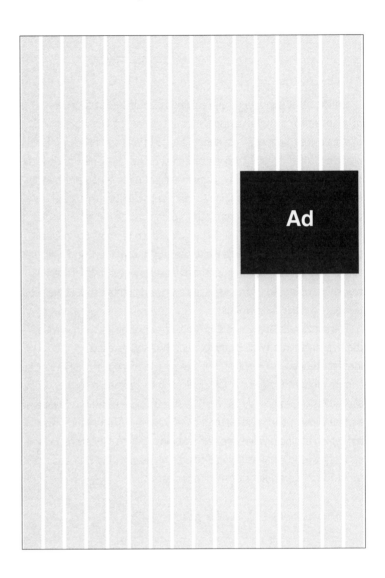

Sixteen units can make for a complex grid, but this arrangement gives us a high level of granularity that will prove useful later on. What's more, because the total number of units is a multiple of four, it conforms to our rule from Chapter 3 that states, "The simpler the grid, the more effective it is." Remember that the idea behind this rule is that grids should be as mathematically useful as possible, i.e., combining units into columns should be based on measurements simple enough to be able to calculate without having to use to a calculator. Sixteen units of 60 pixels wide each, totaling 960 pixels in width, makes for such a mathematically useful framework; we know right away that two units are 120 pixels wide, three units are 180 pixels wide, and so forth.

The mathematical usefulness of this sixteen-unit framework bears out even more when we add the subtlety of gutters. We want to incorporate a gutter between each unit, so that when combined into columns there will always be a gutter available, and mathematically accounted for, to the right of that resulting column. If we establish a gutter of 10 pixels wide and subtract that width from the unit, we're left with sixteen units of 50 pixels wide each, which is an even more straightforward calculus.

ESTABLISHING THE BASELINE GRID

We now have our columnar grid, and it's time to develop our baseline grid. Remember that the baseline is the invisible line on which letterforms rest—the anchor for lines of type. We form a grid by creating a uniform set of these baselines that run from the top of the page to the bottom. The spacing of the lines is determined by our typographic specifications.

A good baseline grid complements larger type elements like headings and subheadings, but baselines are principally obligated with guiding the body text—the text that renders the majority of the content— on a page. Body text on the Web typically runs anywhere from 11 to 14 point in size, though it doesn't take much digging to find designs that use more extreme sizes. Specifying type can be as easy as simply choosing a font size within that range that seems most suitable, but the human eye most comfortably reads (or scans) 60 to 80 characters per line and no more. This is called the line measure, and we typically refer to "wide measures"—typesetting with 80 or more characters per line—as being undesirable because they become difficult to read.

Returning to the columnar grid, we see that the widest area in which we're likely to set text is in the left region, where ten units and nine gutters of space amounts to a width of 590 pixels. That's plenty of room for the main column of text on the article template, which is the template that will likely demand the widest measures of all of our layouts. But even in such a wide column, our text is unlikely to run from edge to edge without some kind of buffer to relieve the visual tension, so we can reduce the width by two units and two gutters, which we'll use as padding. That leaves us eight units and seven gutters for a width of 470 pixels. Even then, we may add additional in-column padding (which we'll discuss later) so the actual width may be closer to 450 pixels.

Georgia Regular 12 pt.
Mr. Phileas Fogg lived, in 1872, at No. 7, Saville Row, Burlington Gardens, the house in which Sheridan died in 1814. He was one of the most noticeable members of the Reform Club, though he seemed always to avoid attracting attention; an enigmatical personage, about whom little was known, except that he was a polished man of the world. People said that he resembled Byron—at least that his head was Byronic; but he was a bearded, tranquil Byron, who might live on a thousand years without growing old.

Georgia Regular 13 pt.
Mr. Phileas Fogg lived, in 1872, at No. 7, Saville Row, Burlington Gardens, the house in which Sheridan died in 1814. He was one of the most noticeable members of the Reform Club, though he seemed always to avoid attracting attention; an enigmatical personage, about whom little was known, except that he was a polished man of the world. People said that he resembled Byron—at least that his head was Byronic; but he was a bearded, tranquil Byron, who might live on a thousand years without growing old.

Georgia Regular 14 pt.
Mr. Phileas Fogg lived, in 1872, at No. 7, Saville Row, Burlington Gardens, the house in which Sheridan died in 1814. He was one of the most noticeable members of the Reform Club, though he seemed always to avoid attracting attention; an enigmatical personage, about whom little was known, except that he was a polished man of the world. People said that he resembled Byron—at least that his head was Byronic; but he was a bearded, tranquil Byron, who might live on a thousand years without growing old.

Setting sample blocks of text helps us determine the right line measure and font size.

The question now is what type size is best suited for such a width? We could use calculation tools, but because every typeface is composed of different metrics the best course of action may be to simply set sample text within such a width and judge the results for ourselves. Typesetting 12-point Georgia Regular, for instance, will yield close to 80 characters per line, while 14-point Georgia Regular will yield just over 60 characters. Some designers—and users—will prefer one or the other size, but for our purposes we'll select 13-point Georgia Regular, which yields roughly 70 characters per line—right in the middle of our sweet spot of 60 to 80 characters per line.

To vet that decision, we also want to set sample text within narrower columns so we can appraise its visual appropriateness. The character count will of course be well short of the maximum measure, but it's still worth making sure that the text will be easily readable in different widths.

Setting type within various other widths helps us vet our choice of font size.

Georgia Regular 13 pt.

Mr. Phileas Fogg lived, in 1872, at No. 7, Saville Row, Burlington Gardens, the house in which Sheridan died in 1814. He was one of the most noticeable members of the Reform Club, though he seemed always to avoid

Georgia Regular 13 pt.

Mr. Phileas Fogg lived, in 1872, at No. 7, Saville Row, Burlington Gardens, the house in which Sheridan died in 1814. He was one of the most noticeable members of the Reform Club, though he seemed always to avoid attracting attention; an enigmatical personage, about whom little was known, except that he was a polished man of the world. People said

Georgia Regular 13 pt.

Mr. Phileas Fogg lived, in 1872, at No. 7, Saville Row, Burlington Gardens, the house in which Sheridan died in 1814. He was one of the most noticeable members of the Reform Club, though he seemed always to avoid attracting attention; an enigmatical personage, about whom little was known, except that he was a polished man of the world. People said that he resembled Byron—at least that his head was Byronic; but he was a bearded, tranquil Byron, who might live on a thousand

The font size in turn lets us determine the line-spacing, which effectively produces the baseline grid. The science of determining the correct line-spacing is really a shadow of the practice of "leading" from traditional typography, which was based on the act of physically adding more space between lines of text in the form of lead slugs. There are a handful of rules of thumb, but no universally accepted guidelines. Visually heavier typefaces demand more line-spacing than lighter ones; typefaces with large, voluminous bodies (especially characters like *B, C,* and *O*) benefit from more leading while typefaces with narrower or smaller bodies need less. There are myriad additional factors to consider: whether a font is italicized, whether it features serifs, how starkly its bold weights contrast with its regular weights, and so on. The short of it is that line-spacing should usually be positive (especially in body text), which is to say 13-point text should always have line-spacing of at least 13 pixels, and it should look good. Too little line-spacing makes it difficult for the eye to parse a paragraph into legible lines, and too much line-spacing makes it difficult for the eye to follow from line to line.

For these purposes, we'll select a line-spacing of 18 pixels, which will allow lines to cohere together nicely into paragraphs. This in effect establishes our baseline grid, with a baseline occurring every 18 pixels starting at the top of the page and running down to the bottom. This grid helps guide us in the placement of typography and other elements, but it's important to remember that it's only a guide. Overly strict adherence to this grid is impractical in Web design, as the added complexity of coding elements to align to both the baseline and columnar grid is hardly worth the effort. The advantages of using a grid in Web design is felt much more acutely when elements align to the columnar grid; put simply, alignment with the baseline grid is too subtle a design detail to benefit most users.

Still, we can refer to the baseline grid to help us make many design decisions that would otherwise be improvised. Paragraph spacing, for example, can be determined by the baseline grid. In print, paragraphs frequently follow one another with no additional leading. But on the Web, where some basic typographic touches such as an indentation on the first line of a paragraph are still not easily implemented, and users tend to scan pages much more quickly than in print, buffering paragraphs with spacing is desirable. We can add a full 18 pixels of line space between paragraphs to maintain consistent visual spacing and to ensure that other elements, when aligned with the baseline grid, are in visual harmony with our paragraphs.

We can also determine the specifications of our headings and subheadings, the HTML elements **H1**, **H2**, **H3**, and so on. **H1**s are typically the most visible text on the page, and they frequently appear apart or distinct from the main body text, so it's not as critical to base those headings on the baseline grid as much as it is to base **H2**s and **H3**s on the baseline grid. These elements should obviously be larger and/or more prominent than the body text, but we're not basing their *font size* directly on the baseline grid but rather their line spacing. For instance, we'll specify our **H2**s at 24 point with a line-spacing of 26 pixels, or two baselines. We could just as well set the type size anywhere between, say 22 point and 30 point, so long as we maintain the line-spacing at 36 pixels. What determines the exact specification is our own visual assessment of how comfortable the type looks within the line-spacing, whether descenders on letterforms such as *g* and *y* overlap text below them, and whether the spacing feels sufficient.

H1 Lorem Ipsum Dolor Sit Amet, Consectetur Adipiscing Elit

H2 Lorem Ipsum Dolor Sit Amet, Consectetur Adipiscing Elit

H3 Lorem Ipsum Dolor Sit Amet, Consectetur Adipiscing Elit

Not all of our text specifications need to map to the baseline grid. Here, H1s are off the grid.

ESTABLISHING THE FIELDS

The baseline grid is essential in establishing fields, rationally determined horizontal divisions on the page that help us in the visual pacing of grouped elements from top to bottom. Fields can be useful for sizing the approximate space necessary for the branding and navigation at the top of the page, for example, or estimating the appropriate space for content that is intended to sit higher on the page than other content.

In print design, we might create fields by dividing the page into a number of discrete horizontal regions, allowing us to achieve a precise balance of elements from top to bottom. On the Web though, the height of the page is usually an unknown quantity. One page can fit all of its elements and content in the "above the fold" area, allowing the user to access all content without scrolling, while another page within the same website might have a page that's so long it requires seemingly interminable scrolling. Creating a design framework that divides these pages into thirds, for example, is impractical since the resulting thirds would be wildly inconsistent.

Still, the concept of fields can help us establish a visual rhythm along this unpredictable axis. Fields of a fixed height running from top to bottom can serve as guidelines along which we can place key elements; at the same time, we can ignore these guidelines at will.

How do we determine the correct height for these fields? The answer is to use the golden ratio. Sort of. Rather than fully calculating the true ideal measurements for these regions using the golden ratio in all its complexities, we can acknowledge the limited resolution of our computer screens and therefore justify using a simplified form of the golden ratio—the relatively round number of 1.618—to determine an approximation. This is as simple as dividing the width of our page, 960 pixels, by the number 1.618, which yields a value of approximately 593.

What this tells us is that a rectangle of 960 pixels wide by 593 pixels tall is roughly consistent with the golden ratio; if we place that rectangle at the top of the page, its bottom edge demarcates a field for us—or nearly does. Within our baseline grid, the closest baseline occurs at 594 pixels, or 33 baselines down from the top. Again, this is an exercise in approximations, so that number is entirely acceptable for our purposes: our horizontal field will occur every 594 pixels from the top of the page.

The golden ratio helps us determine the height of our fields.

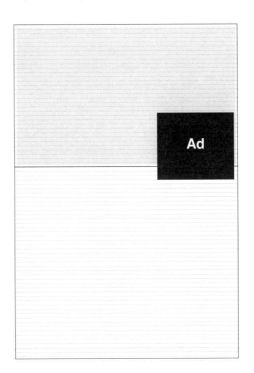

It's also worth noting that within this rectangle we can form a square of 594 pixels on each side, and its right edge roughly aligns with a significant columnar division in the page that we've created. This is a matter of happenstance only; there's no mathematical design that helped us arrive at this happy coincidence, but it still serves as a useful confirmation that the grid is solidly built.

Demarcating a field at every 594 pixels leaves many gaps in design guidance. The unfortunate truth of many web pages is that they're replete with elements that need to find a home on the page, many too varied in size to depend on a guideline only once every 594 pixels. What we want from our grid, particularly our baseline grid, is an infrastructure of visual hints as to where we might align any given element with the knowledge that it fits neatly into our overarching sense of order.

Of course, we could use our 18-pixel baseline grid and align elements on any of the hundreds of baselines that occur on a page, but that presents too many guides. What we need is something in between, something roughly equivalent to our columnar grid.

This can be easily achieved by using the rule of thirds to further refine our fields. If we divide the 594-pixel height by three (remembering that three is a particularly effective divisor), we create divisions of 198 pixels each along the baseline grid. By using a full baseline as a visual gutter between each of the thirds, we create fields of 180 pixels each, or ten baselines each.

Fields applied throughout the length of the page.

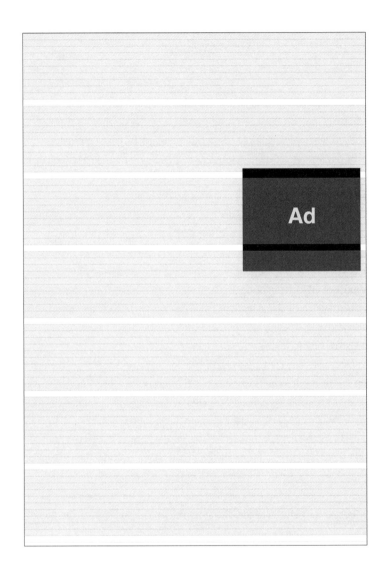

It's important to note that the baseline grid, even more than the columnar grid, is only a set of guidelines, and is not meant to be strictly obeyed. Again, there are too many elements on most Web pages to affix or align each one to the baseline grid. Doing so would require a mathematical rigor that, if it can be achieved, might produce rationally exact measurements and placements but will most likely be something less than elegant. The result would be a design driven by math, rather than a design that uses math to create an elegant product. What's more, the effort required to remain completely true to the baseline is likely to exceed its usefulness to the designer and the user. What's important here is to build a sound grid foundation that can provide guidance where necessary, while at the same time reserving the right to disregard it. Any grid is a series of suggestions, and it's the designer's responsibility to accept them or disregard them.

DESIGNING THE PAGE TEMPLATE

With the basic grid completed, we can begin to design the actual interface for our site. First we'll want to establish the placement of the core elements, the ones that appear persistently throughout the site: the search box, navigation, account log-in and sign-up l inks, and, of course, the brand.

To do this, we'll divide the page into two major regions, one for the main content and one for the ad unit and secondary content. By combining six units on the right side of the page we create an create a column that can house our advertising unit, leaving ten columns to the left for our main text column.

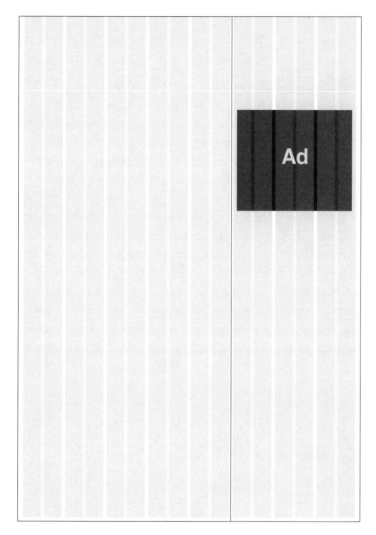

Our page template starts with a simple division of the page into major regions.

We'll use some artistic license here and place the Designery.us logo in the far right column, prominently at the top of the page. This off-kilter presentation is congruent with the design-friendly sensibilities of the audience. Placing it on the right also allows us to display the logo at a consistently larger size than if we had placed it on the left side, where it would compete for space with each page's primary headline and content.

What's more, its placement in this position helps resolve a problem that occurs frequently in website design: the far-right column is commonly overlooked. Many web users pay little attention to this region of the page, and with good reason: website publishers frequently use it as a kind of dumping ground for advertisements and promotional items. Displaying the Designery.us logo at the top of this region can help mitigate that phenomenon, as its prominence can visually activate the space.

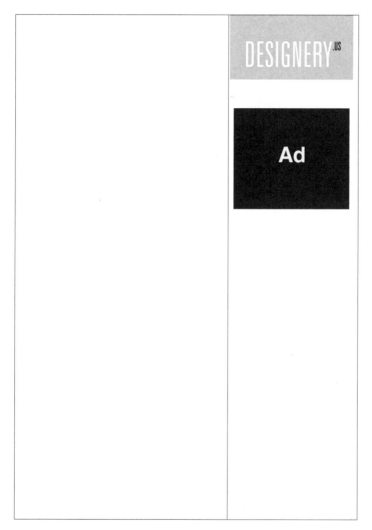

Placing our logo at the top right for an off-kilter presentation.

We can further energize this region by including additional elements that have real value for the user. For example, the user's profile area, which includes his logged-in state and notifications of his messages and updates, can be placed just below the logo. This is a prominent position for elements that communicate directly relevant information to the user (in contrast to the ad unit and the links to peripheral content that are more commonly found in this part of the page), which increases the overall value of this far-right region and decreases the likelihood that it will be ignored.

Note that this information is divided up into two short columns. Each is left-aligned with the columnar grid, of course, and the text is aligned with the baseline grid. The avatar icon is also aligned with the baseline grid.

We don't want to relegate all of the critical elements to that far-right region, of course. In fact, with the logo at the right, it's even more important that our navigation be easily accessed from the left side of the page. So we'll run the navigational elements along the top edge where users will be sure to spot them.

Adding account elements just below the logo.

The account elements are aligned with our grid.

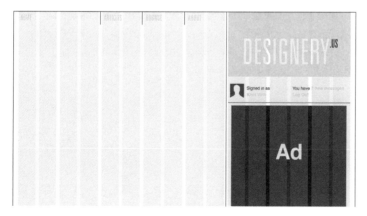

Placing our navigation elements across the top of the page.

Looking at the grid, there are ten units in this region, which can be consolidated into five columns of two units each. Each column would measure 110 pixels wide, a comfortable amount of space for navigational buttons. However, our wireframe shows only three navigational elements: Home, Articles, and Browse (the Profile section now appears at the far right). We can promote the About Designery link that our wireframe suggests should appear in the footer to the level of the top navigation, reasoning that it's too important to be left so far down the page. This gives us a total of four navigational elements. That still leaves one column blank, but we can address that by giving the Home link—usually the most important of all navigational links—a double-wide space of four units, or 230 pixels. This makes the Home link particularly prominent and findable without requiring us to make it too visually loud.

Note also that the navigational links do not align with the baseline. The type is just a bit too tall to fit comfortably in our baseline grid without consuming more space than is truly necessary. Instead, we'll make the height of the navigation button—the overall area in which the link resides—two baselines, or 36 pixels, tall, and center the text vertically within that area. We define the height of those areas with a vertical divider line.

Using the baseline grid to guide the height of these navigation items also helps us determine the rollover states of these items. When the user mouses over any of the items, a background color will appear to emphasize their clickability.

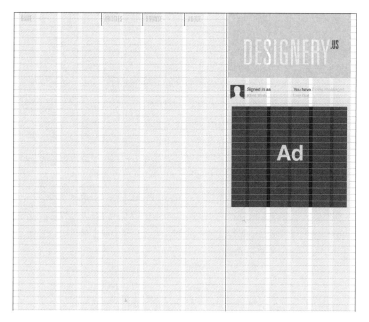

The type in the navigational elements does not align with the baseline grid.

Rollover states for the navigational elements.

This is a good opportunity to reiterate the importance of spacing in grid-based design. Notice that the navigation links do not align with the left edge of the column. In fact, none of the text we've placed so far (or will place) fully aligns with the left edges of its respective column. Every piece of text is nudged in slightly from those edges by 5 pixels.

The reason we do this is that we must account for the behavior of these text items. In print design, elements are more commonly fully aligned with their column edges, but they remain fixed in place and rarely have different states.

Aligning elements with their column edges looks good.

This is an aesthetically unimpeachable layout technique but it does not contend with rollover states, which are common on the Web for functional or link text. This is what fundamentally distinguishes interaction design from its antecedents in print: the digital designer must account for behaviors.

On the Web, a link or text button in its default state might look like simple text on a plain background, but it often carries additional behaviors. On rollover, for instance, a colored background box is revealed as part of the link.

But it presents problems when we create different behavioral states.

As you can see from this example, text that fully aligns with the column edge presents problems. On rollover, the text crashes into the left edge. We can adjust it in the rollover state—that is, nudge it a few pixels to the right of the column edge—to make it more aesthetically pleasing and accommodate that behavior. But to have the text placed at one location and its rollover state placed in another location can be disconcerting, especially if a user rolls on and off a link quickly or repeatedly. The same text would jump erratically between spots. It's wisest to make the placement for both the default and rollover states consistent; that is, the text placement for the default state should be the same as the text placement for the rollover state.

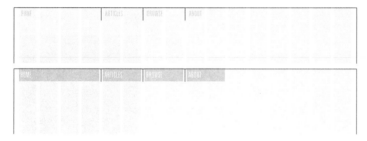

Instead, place elements a few pixels away from the column edges.

The implication here is not just that link text should be placed a few pixels away from column edges, but rather that *all text* should be padded in this way. Having a mix of placements—some at the column edge and others nudged in—will create visual disarray, to begin with. At the same time, it's difficult to know what text will function as links and what text will not, so it's safest to assume that all text, at some point or another, has the potential to assume additional behaviors.

Returning to our page template, we'll also add the search box along the same axis as the navigation links. Search is frequently used as a form of navigation, and presenting it inline with the navigation creates a logical organization, though in this case we'll place search above the Designery logo back in the far-right region. We'll also use some artistic license to design a slightly unusual search box, one that looks like a blank line rather than a box.

Adding the search box above the logo.

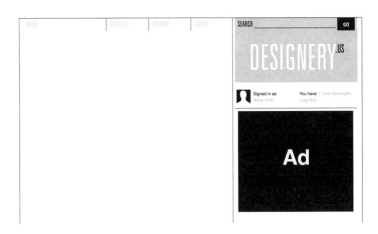

Finally, we have the footer to include in the template. Different schools of web design argue that footers can be simple and incidental or very complex and substantial. Either approach is valid, but in this case we'll favor a simpler footer. Using alignments with our grid, we can include the copyright information at the left, then a string of secondary navigational links indented at about four units from the left. Though the placement of these two elements echoes the double-wide Home link and the other navigational links at the top, it's not entirely necessary to expressly match the columnar structure in the main body of the page. So long as the elements in the footer are aligned with elements of the grid, that should be enough.

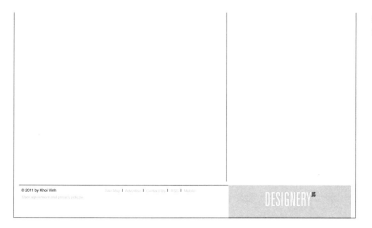

Adding the footer to the page.

The completed page template.

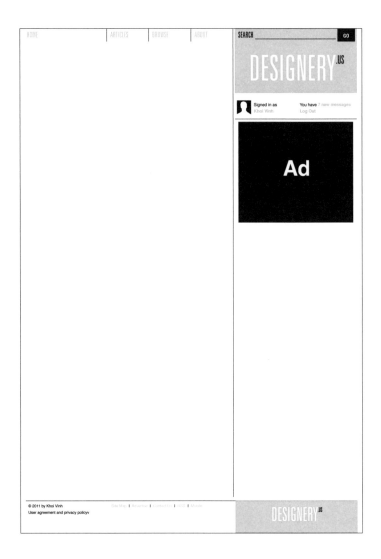

That said, we can echo the far-right region of the main part of the page with a bit of Designery branding. This subtly emphasizes the unusual placement of the logo in the far-right column.

That completes the design of our basic template. It establishes a standard set of elements to be used throughout the site, but of course we should keep in mind that any element can be modified to produce the best possible total user experience. In the following projects, we'll see where and when it's appropriate to make those kinds of changes.

PROJECT 1: ARTICLE PAGE

When designing a website, many designers begin with the home page template, a logical starting point because the home page can establish so much of the site's aesthetic tone. Oftentimes, though, the home page can present so unique a challenge that it keeps us from reaching our bigger goal: as we start the design process, we want to solve as many of the most wide-reaching problems as early as we can.

There's also the argument that the home page is the most prominent page on the site, the face and gateway to the content. Again, this is a completely valid argument, but in the direct access world of the Web, it's the content itself (and not the gateway to that content) that often matters most. The home page, after all, is usually an index of content. On the other hand, the kind of pages that contain the content— like the product page on a shopping site, or like the article page on a content site—attract the most attention from search engines, get forwarded via email, and make the rounds on social networks.

For those reasons, we'll use the basic template we've designed to first tackle the article page template. Of course, we'll base our design on the requirements in this wireframe:

Designery.us

Home	Articles	Browse	Profile

Welcome back, Khoi

7 Messages | LOG-OUT

Search [   ] SEARCH

Previous Article

Next Article

2010-MM-DD

Article Headline Goes Here

A brief summary of the article goes here. Lorem ipsum dolor sit amet, consectetur adipisicing elit, sed do eiusmod tempor incididunt ut labore et dolore magna aliqua. Ut enim ad minim veniam.

○ PRINT   ○ EMAIL   ○ SHARE

By John Doe
Editor

Lorem ipsum dolor sit amet, consectetur adipiscing elit. Vivamus quis felis lectus. Ut ac leo justo. Cras adipiscing nulla quis erat convallis tincidunt. Ut dapibus molestie eros, vitae feugiat ligula gravida eget. Integer in nulla at lectus blandit commodo sed vitae tortor.

A caption for this large image goes here.

Integer suscipit tincidunt augue, sit amet auctor enim tempus et. Donec elementum interdum pretium. Duis quis libero orci. Morbi ut dui turpis, sed viverra tellus. Quisque sollicitudin lectus eget nisi laoreet condimentum. Suspendisse ultrices lobortis ipsum sed facilisis. Cras malesuada arcu eget leo commodo vitae commodo dolor dictum. Nulla facilisi. Pellentesque habitant morbi tristique senectus et netus et malesuada fames ac turpis egestas. Morbi elit ante, porttitor vel lobortis id, viverra ac eros.

Cras tincidunt iaculis risus id faucibus. Sed sed justo id quam scelerisque euismod ac non ante. Nunc ullamcorper nisl vitae mi ultrices sit amet laoreet odio hendrerit. Nunc et nisi eu nisi eleifend imperdiet et quis dolor. Donec vitae lacus interdum ipsum fringilla luctus. ■

Big Ad

Recent Articles

Article One Headline
By Jane Smith

Article Two Headline
By Don Jones

Recent Projects

Project Name

Project Name

Subscribe to Our Email Newsletter

Email [   ]

GO

About Designery | Contact Us | ○ RSS Feed | Legal Notices   © 2011 by Khoi Vinh

The primary component of this page is, of course, the large column of text that houses the content and that is an ideal fit for the left-hand region of our basic template. We can quickly flow sample content into that left-hand region using the type specifications we've already established to get a sense of how this works.

Recall that when we established our type specifications, we determined that the widest column our text would run in would be made up of eight units—even though we have ten units here. This preserves the comfortable line measure (number of characters appearing per line) for reading.

In this preliminary layout, the eight-unit column is flanked by empty units that create a visual margin. While this is acceptable, content is usually best served by appearing as far left as reasonably possible, so we'll create a bit of a design flourish in the middle of the page: we'll shift the eight-unit column to the left and create a two-unit gutter that will remain relatively empty.

This runs counter to the impulse to take advantage of every bit of space possible to deliver information as efficiently as possible. But in fact carving out an area that remains relatively empty can aid the overall page by allowing it to breathe visually. Aesthetically speaking, it's also in keeping with the large amount of negative space that we've created at the top of the page.

Our wireframe also calls for a few other major elements: a navigation mechanism that allows users to jump from article to article, a list of recent articles, a list of recent projects, and an email subscription sign-up form.

It would be impractical to stack all these elements in the right-hand region, as suggested in the wireframe. As elements intended to help users find additional content or services, we don't want users to have to encounter them linearly, which would be the case if a user had to scroll further down the page before seeing them one by one. Instead, we want as many of them to appear as close to the top of the page as is reasonable. To do that, we'll subdivide that right-hand region into columns by simply dividing that six-unit area into two columns of three units each.

This lets us place several of these elements relatively high on the page without any one of them forcing the others too far down the page. Let's start with the lists of articles and projects; they can appear side by side, directly below the ad unit.

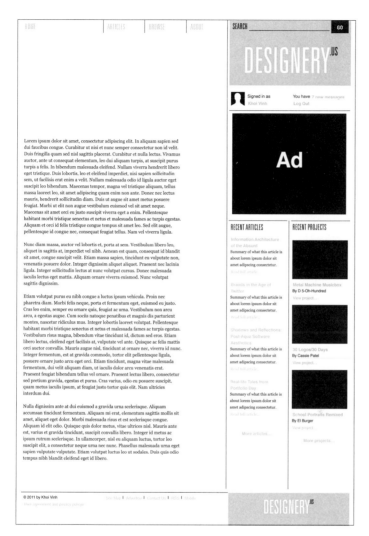

The headings on these elements follow approximately the same style as the navigation that we created earlier: they also use our brand typeface, Univers, and simply add a thin rule above the heading text. The text itself is centered vertically within two baselines, again like the navigation. These headings are fairly minor details, and it makes sense to reuse type specifications from elsewhere in the design; the fewer type styles we have, the more orderly the overall layout appears.

Placing these two lists below the ad is straightforward, but if we then turn to the email subscription form, we realize that if it comes after these two lists of items it would appear too far down the page for many users to notice. Since it doesn't require a great deal of height, we can promote it to a higher position.

This leaves the article-to-article navigation. This too can take advantage of the two columns we've created in the right region, with a box in the left column serving as a link to the previous article and a box in the right region serving as a link to the next article. This navigation requires more prominence than the other items we've placed in this region, though. Navigation is generally more critical than promotional content. If designed properly, it appears and performs consistently and in congruence with user expectations, and so becomes critical to the utility of the site. For those reasons we'll place these navigation links above the ad unit, in a spot where users can always find them.

Lorem ipsum dolor sit amet, consectetur adipiscing elit. In aliquam sapien sed dui faucibus congue. Curabitur ut nisi et nunc semper consectetur non id velit. Duis fringilla quam sed nisl sagittis placerat. Curabitur et nulla lectus. Vivamus auctor, ante ut consequat elementum, leo dui aliquam turpis, at suscipit purus turpis a felis. In bibendum malesuada eleifend. Nullam viverra hendrerit libero eget tristique. Duis lobortis, leo et eleifend imperdiet, nisi sapien sollicitudin sem, ut facilisis erat enim a velit. Nullam malesuada odio id ligula auctor eget suscipit leo bibendum. Maecenas tempor, magna vel tristique aliquam, tellus massa laoreet leo, sit amet adipiscing quam enim non ante. Donec nec lectus mauris, hendrerit sollicitudin diam. Duis at augue sit amet metus posuere feugiat. Morbi ut elit non augue vestibulum euismod vel sit amet neque. Maecenas sit amet orci eu justo suscipit viverra eget a enim. Pellentesque habitant morbi tristique senectus et netus et malesuada fames ac turpis egestas. Aliquam et orci id felis tristique congue tempus sit amet leo. Sed elit augue, pellentesque id congue nec, consequat feugiat tellus. Nam vel viverra ligula.

Nunc diam massa, auctor vel lobortis et, porta at sem. Vestibulum libero leo, aliquet in sagittis at, imperdiet vel nibh. Aenean est quam, consequat id blandit sit amet, congue suscipit velit. Etiam massa sapien, tincidunt eu vulputate non, venenatis posuere dolor. Integer dignissim aliquet aliquet. Praesent nec lacinia ligula. Integer sollicitudin lectus at nunc volutpat cursus. Donec malesuada iaculis lectus eget mattis. Aliquam ornare viverra euismod. Nunc volutpat sagittis dignissim.

Etiam volutpat purus eu nibh congue a luctus ipsum vehicula. Proin nec pharetra diam. Morbi felis neque, porta et fermentum eget, euismod eu justo. Cras leo enim, semper ut ornare quis, feugiat ac urna. Vestibulum non arcu arcu, a egestas augue. Cum sociis natoque penatibus et magnis dis parturient montes, nascetur ridiculus mus. Integer lobortis laoreet volutpat. Pellentesque habitant morbi tristique senectus et netus et malesuada fames ac turpis egestas. Vestibulum risus magna, bibendum vitae tincidunt id, dictum sed eros. Etiam libero lectus, eleifend eget facilisis at, vulputate vel ante. Quisque ac felis mattis orci auctor convallis. Mauris augue nisi, tincidunt at ornare nec, viverra id nunc. Integer fermentum, est at gravida commodo, tortor elit pellentesque ligula, posuere ornare justo arcu eget orci. Etiam tincidunt, magna vitae malesuada fermentum, dui velit aliquam diam, ut iaculis dolor arcu venenatis erat. Praesent feugiat bibendum tellus vel ornare. Praesent lectus libero, consectetur sed pretium gravida, egestas et purus. Cras varius, odio eu posuere suscipit, quam metus iaculis ipsum, at feugiat justo tortor quis elit. Nam ultricies interdum dui.

Nulla dignissim ante at dui euismod a gravida urna suscipit. Aliquam accumsan tincidunt fermentum. Aliquam mi erat, elementum sagittis mollis sit amet, aliquet eget dolor. Morbi malesuada risus et est scelerisque congue. Aliquam id elit odio. Quisque quis dolor metus, vitae ultrices nisl. Mauris ante est, varius et gravida tincidunt, suscipit convallis libero. Integer id metus ac ipsum rutrum scelerisque. In ullamcorper, nisl eu aliquam luctus, tortor leo suscipit elit, a consectetur neque urna nec nunc. Phasellus malesuada urna eget sapien vulputate vulputate. Etiam volutpat luctus leo ut sodales. Duis quis odio tempus nibh blandit eleifend eget id libero.

The article-to-article navigation requires more prominence, so it's placed above the ad.

Most of our elements are now in place on the page, and we can turn our attention to some of the smaller details. Actually, the next detail is smaller but still significant: the headline and byline area of the article.

In our design of the basic template, we've already established the type specifications for our **H2** headings, but here we need to determine specifications for the headline as an **H1** style. Aside from the logo, this will be the most prominent type on the page. (In fact, for many users, especially those entering the site through an article, the headline may need to be even more prominent than the logo.)

Our 18-pixel baseline grid can help us determine a size relatively quickly if we use a multiple of 18 to determine the line-height. Three baselines, or 54 pixels, is too large, so we'll use two baselines, or 36 pixels. With a line-height of 36 pixels, we'll want the text to be slightly smaller, and using a sans-serif font like Arial or Helvetica, we can set the size at 34 point to achieve a nice balance between size and line-spacing.

We'll set the byline, date, and summary of the article at 12 point on the baseline grid, again in a sans-serif font. Note that by using sans-serif typography for this kind of metainformation as well as for many of the elements we've already placed on the page, we're establishing a convention where serif fonts are reserved for the longer blocks of text that make up the content itself.

We can use the same typographic approach for the print, email, and share links that need to appear near the top of the article. These three items should be placed somewhere easily findable but inconspicuous, and here we can use the negative space we've created at the right of the body text for that purpose. We'll place the links to the right of the byline and the summary, within that negative space. The links are relatively small, so they'll remain unobtrusive in size. But their placement in this column—surrounded by so much space above and below— will make them noticeable when the user scans the page for them.

*Adding type styles
for the title, byline, and
summary elements
at the top of the article.*

Our wireframe specifies that the body of the article will usually contain illustrations and a caption, and there are additional elements that we need to account for: block quotes and lists that might appear in the text.

Images are easy enough to place in the flow of the text column. We'll also create a caption style that will follow our concept of metatext appearing in a sans-serif font. To keep it distinct from the main text, we'll make it 1 point smaller and set it in a lighter shade of gray. This caption appears directly beneath the image, and we'll skip a baseline before resuming the article.

Block quotes also need to be distinguished from the main text, but in a different way; rather than functioning as a kind of metainformation, block quotes are integral to the narrative within the text. We'll do this by using an italic version of the serif font in the body and indenting the entire block quote paragraph by one unit.

Adding a blockquote style to the body.

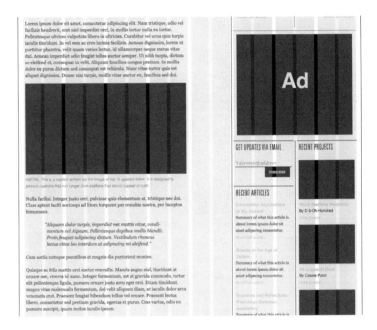

We'll use a similar indentation for a list style within the text. The items themselves will be indented by one unit, but the bullets for the lists—whether numeric (in the case of ordered lists) or dingbats (in the case of unordered lists)—are right-aligned with the left edge of that second unit. If an ordered list were to get lengthy and three-digit list item numbers were needed, the numbers would grow to the *left*, rather than to the right, thereby protecting the integrity of the entire list's indentation along the columnar grid.

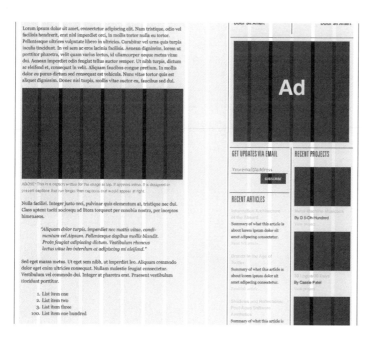

Adding a list style to the body.

Finally, we'll add a set of tools that allow the user to take action on the article—print, email, and share—to the header area of the page. This is a fairly minor element, but it's important that it occurs in a subtle but prominent location as many users will look for it. We can take advantage of the empty column that we created to the right of the text and to the left of the advertising unit for this purpose; by placing the article tools near the top of this column, they can visually activate that vertical space while calling attention to themselves.

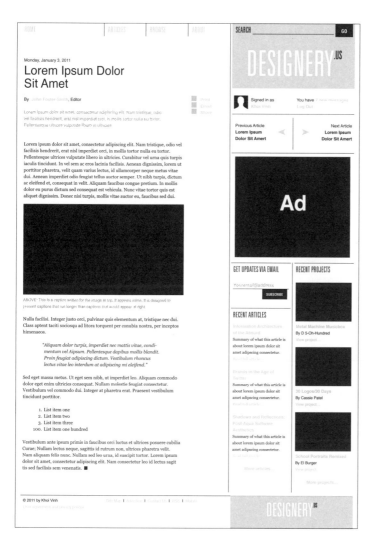

PROJECT 2: CATEGORY PAGE

As we push forward and design further templates, we'll continue to borrow patterns for the placement, arrangement, and configuration of page elements from the article template. That's how we maintain consistency within a design system. At the same time, we'll be inventing new patterns and potentially revising some of the old ones—different templates will call for different elements, and so we'll remain flexible about the execution of our ideas.

Take our next template, the category page, as an example. This page offers a menu of projects and people to choose from within the hypothetical social network of Designery.us; it presents a series of thumbnails of people and projects that invite the user to sample the breadth and depth of the site. In our wireframes, the category page shows two major regions in a two-thirds/one-third layout. At first glance, this seems a natural fit for the basic arrangement we created for the article page.

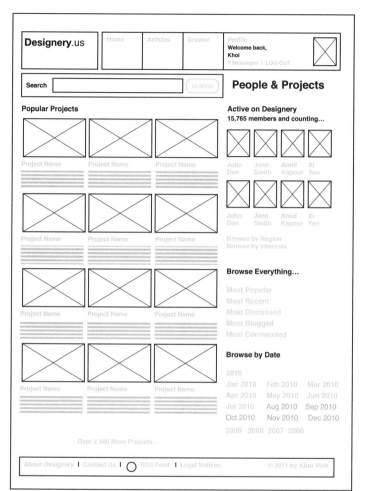

The wireframe for our category page.

Our thumbnail sketch of the layout for this page.

If we were to simply echo that article page, we'd be creating a consistent experience, which is a good thing. However, we'd also be missing an opportunity to create a better design. The goals that a user has in mind when he encounters this page are different from those he has in mind when he encounters an article. In the latter case, he is principally concerned with reading an article, immersing himself in one train of thought, and only secondarily concerned about straying further afield to see what else Designery.us has to offer. In the case of the category page, the user is primarily looking to explore what the site has to offer and who else is engaged with its content and features; he doesn't want to focus on one idea, he wants to survey all the ideas—or the most interesting ideas—available on the site.

To that end, it would actually be a disservice to simply reuse our layout from the article page. Instead, we want to create a new kind of layout that addresses the specific needs of this particular template while remaining consistent with the overall design that we began to create with that template. That mission is made significantly easier by building our new Category template design on the same sturdy grid foundation we've already established.

Instead of a two-thirds/one-third layout, we can imagine a more symmetrical layout where the projects are arranged in two columns down the middle of the page and flanked with their descriptive text. We can even extend that symmetrical approach to the other items on the page: the elements in the right-hand region on our wireframe can be arranged in three symmetrical columns as well. A rough thumbnail sketch can help us work out these notions:

Although we're using three columns to organize the text, the division between columns is less pronounced than the division between the two-thirds region and the one-third region from our article page. In a sense, we want all of the columns to act together as a single region, even if they'll be segregated from one another.

To do this, we'll simply extend the dividing rule that runs under the log-in section across the entire expanse of the page. This interrupts the downward visual thrust of the branding area and helps demarcate a "top of the page." This is where the title of the page will go. And the area that falls under this line is now more of a blank slate, undisturbed by the asymmetrical branding above it.

By extending the rule beneath the account elements, we create a different region dynamic on the page.

Our sketch suggests that the thumbnails for our projects should occupy a fairly wide middle region, two columns side-by-side. We can consolidate eight units from our 16-unit grid to form that region, and flank it with four units on each side.

In effect, this is the general dynamic of the page: a strong central region offset by the branding in the top right. As we add the other elements to the page, we want to keep this in mind and avoid disrupting that dynamic.

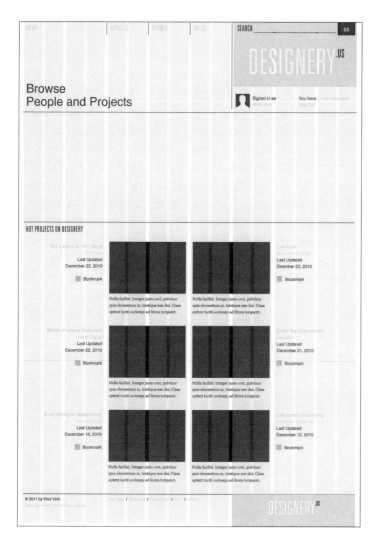

The collection of avatar icons of Designery.us users, for instance, can be placed right above the project thumbnails. We can tie their size directly into our grid by making them exactly one unit in size: 50 x 50 pixels. This allows us to place plenty of thumbnails in this section—eight across and four down. And since this is just a sampling of the thousands of users on Designery.us, we can create a link to find more people in the bottom right corner by combining slots for two thumbnails into one.

One problem now presents itself. Identifying users by avatar icons alone can be difficult. Though it's not uncommon on the Web to display lists of users in this icon-only fashion, it's preferable to create a mechanism for revealing the names attached to each icon. Normally that can be done by simply rolling over the icon to reveal the name as text label, but here we can be more creative.

By carving out a display area within the grid of icons, we can let users enlarge the thumbnails in place. Clicking on one of the surrounding icons would enlarge it in this display area and reveal that user's name and additional information.

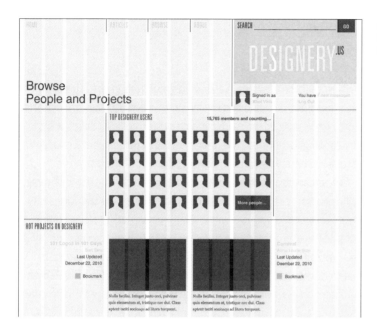

A gallery of user avatar icons placed directly above the projects.

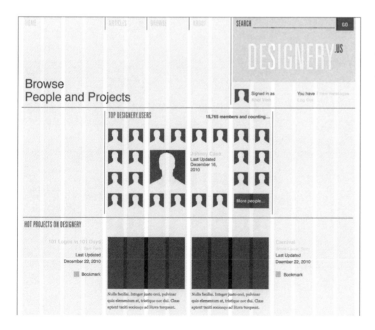

We can use the grid to design a mechanism for revealing the names attached to each avatar icon.

Note that the enlarged avatar is 110 x 110 pixels in size. This allows it to conform to the grid and remain proportional to the smaller avatar icons. This is one of the more pleasing side effects of using a well-developed grid: at times, the design seems to guide itself, without requiring arbitrary design decisions.

We can apply a similar solution to the date archives. The wireframe calls for a sort of miniature, year-by-year browser; the user clicks on a year and a list of months within that year appears in place. To the right of the user avatars, we have four units that we can use for this. Rather than arrange the years horizontally, as suggested in the wireframe, we can arrange them vertically, creating a list of years that can function as navigation. When the user clicks on a year, the months appear to the right of it within the remaining three units. In practice, because every year has the same months, the right-hand side won't change much, but the overall browsing interface should still be intuitive for nearly everyone.

Adding the date browser in the top-right corner.

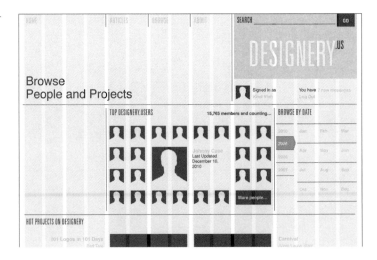

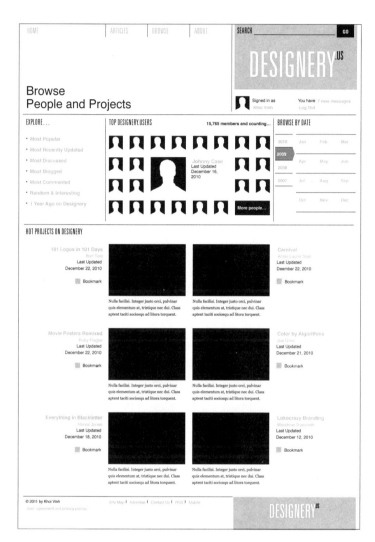

The final category page design.

Finally, we can place the list of Explore links to the left of the avatar icons. This is very straightforward, literally just a list of links. Oftentimes simplest is best.

Throughout the process of assembling this design, there's been no mention of the baseline grid, but in fact, if we take a look at the placement of the elements we can see that they are in alignment with the baselines.

A look at the category page design with the baseline grid.

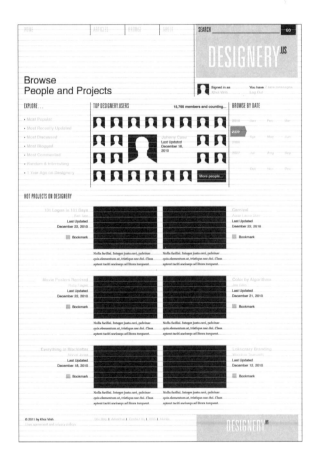

In many ways, the placement of elements on the baseline grid on this page is determined by the subheads (Explore, Top Designery.users, Browse by Date and Hot Projects on Designery). As established on the article template, the rules that appear above each subhead are aligned to a baseline, the subhead text itself is aligned vertically between two baselines, and one additional baseline is skipped before content beneath the baseline appears.

Stepping back from the completed design we can see that the general dynamic of the page is quite pleasing. There is a strong symmetry to the page as seen in the project thumbnails with their flanking pieces of textual information, but there is a lot of asymmetry at work too: the off-center large avatar, the text list on the left that is not quite counterbalanced by the date browser to the right, and the logo at the top right. The page successfully echoes the article template in terms of maintaining a clear aesthetic link (and maintaining the branding and typographic styles), while also addressing the distinct challenges of this category page.

Finally, we'll add a set of tools that allow the user to take action on the article—print, email, and share—to the header area of the page. This is a fairly minor element, but it's important that it occurs in a subtle but prominent location as many users will look for it. We can take advantage of the empty column that we created to the right of the text and to the left of the advertising unit for this purpose; by placing the article tools near the top of this column, they can visually activate that vertical space while calling attention to themselves.

PROJECT 3: PROFILE PAGE

Up next is the user profile page for Designery.us. Our wireframe suggests that in many ways it's similar to the category page—it provides a high-level view of many different kinds of content, rather than a presentation of just one particular piece of content.

At the same time, it obviously offers a more narrow focus than the category page in that it presents the biography and network activity of a single user. Where the category page design was meant to be expansive in its survey of activity across the site, the layout for this profile page should be more intimate.

A quick thumbnail sketch emphasizes the user's personal information at the top of the page as the principal element in the design, occupying a region of its own. Additional information, like the user's friends, projects, and activity, follows underneath, much like extensions of the personal information at the top.

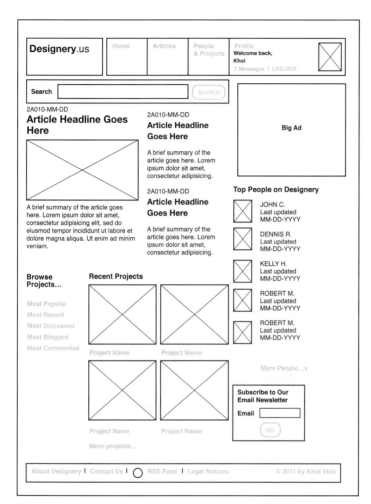

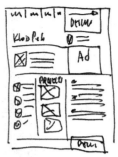

At left, the wireframe for the profile page and above, the thumbnail sketch for its design.

This layout suggests a hybrid of the two-thirds/one-third layout from the article page and the symmetrical layout from the category page. It still allows our big ad to form a region of its own at the far right, but it borrows from the layout of the category page by carving out an area at the top that is horizontally congruent with the same ad. In fact, you can look at the basic architecture of this layout as an extension of the dimensions of the ad unit:

The basic architecture of the page is an extension of the dimensions of the ad unit.

With this basic arrangement in place, we can begin to work the content into the regions. The personal information at the top is the obvious place to start, because it needs to command the most attention on the page. Other users who arrive at this page must recognize immediately that it is devoted to one particular user, and that user's name and image must be prominent. At the same time, it must also provide the user's biographic details in a quick, easy to read form. The goal of the page is to allow others to quickly get a sense of who this person is.

Again, we'll borrow from the convention we established on the category page by extending the dividing rule that runs under the log-in section across the expanse of the page. As with the category page design, this allows us to carve out a fairly spacious region at the top of the page for the title. Unlike the category page design, we're not really using this line to interrupt the downward visual thrust of the branding area.

In fact, we're depending on that downward visual thrust to help define the right-most column. Here that line defines the top portion of a new region that extends the dimension of the ad unit. (Also recall there was no ad unit on the category page.) We can complete the thought by extending a dividing rule just below the big ad, again across the entire page.

Adding divider rules to define the page.

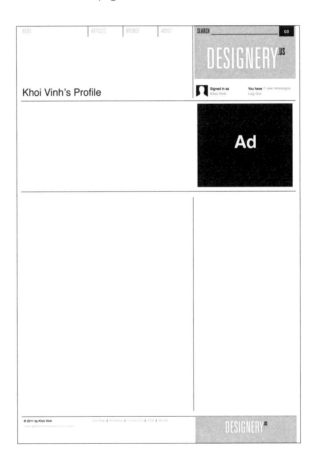

How we use this space is now the question. We could place the avatar icon for the user next to the title of the page for maximum impact, as shown.

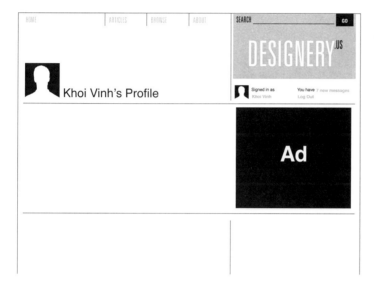

One possible placement for the user's avatar icon.

However, that presents two problems. First, it bumps the user's name a few units to the right. That creates a slight hurdle for viewers scanning for this user's name. Much like the headline on our article page design—and any **H1** text that functions as the most critical piece of information on the page—it's helpful to keep the name as far left as possible for easy legibility.

Our second problem is that if we place the image outside the region we've created just below the title, we have scant few elements to put in that region. Recall that shorter lines are easier to read, especially with information that is meant to be consumed quickly, such as the biographical information we're designing now. Without the avatar icon in that area, the text would need to run in longer line measures (characters per line). Some of the bits of information are quite short, as well, leaving significant negative space. While the look and feel we've established thus far has generally not shied away from using negative space, our strategy is not simply to create as much of it as we can, but rather to use it purposefully and judiciously. By contrast, this kind of negative space feels unintentional and disorderly.

All of this argues for placing the icon below the title. Doing so takes up two units of width and effectively creates a narrower column for the biographical information. In fact, we can further narrow that column by creating another sub-column in which we can place the label for each bit of biographical data. That consumes two additional units of width, and leaves us with six units within which we can run the actual information.

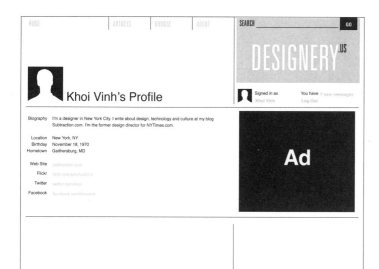

With the avatar icon at the top, the information below feels disorderly.

A different placement for the avatar information makes more sense.

As you can see, this presentation makes much more sense. The avatar icon is close to the profile name at the top of the page, but it also breaks up the space within the region below. The labels hang to the left of the actual information, which makes the data more easily scannable. And the biographical information resides in a narrower, more comfortable-to-read column.

As a finishing touch for this region, we'll also add links for the Send message and Add as a Friend functionality just below the avatar. Again, this adjacency works well; it comes just below the elements that allow another user to identify who this user is—a perfect spot to place links that enable another user to take action on that information.

Below the biographical information, we're confronted with our familiar two-thirds/one-third division of the page. As it happens, we also have three different kinds of content to place here: the user's friends, projects, and activity. Having three kinds of content suggests that we also divide this region into three, echoing the symmetry we created on the category page.

However, the far-right column has already been defined to some extent by the ad above it. Though not impossible, it would be uncomfortable to reduce its width to precisely echo the three-column construction from the category page. (Recall that we created this by setting up two columns of four units each flanking a single column of eight units.)

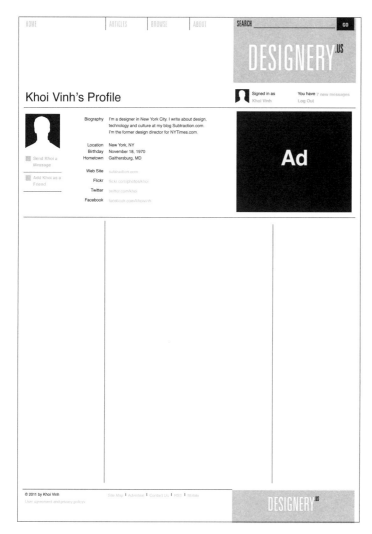

Lower on the page, we might divide the page into three equal regions, echoing the symmetry from the category page.

Here we can remain consistent without being rote. We can still create three columns in the lower portion of the page, but they can be responsive to the specific requirements of this particular design problem rather than a replication of another design problem.

To do this we'll maintain the far-right column's six-unit width. That leaves us with ten units to the left. From these, we'll combine four units to create a left-hand column and six units to create a middle column. The resulting structure is shown on the opposite page.

Though not perfectly symmetrical, we can use the power of the content itself to help this arrangement echo the layout of the category page. We have three kinds of content here but the one with the most visual impact is the details of this user's projects, which are represented by thumbnail pictures. If we place these in the middle column, we can create a semblance of symmetry down what is visually (if not math-ematically) the center of the page.

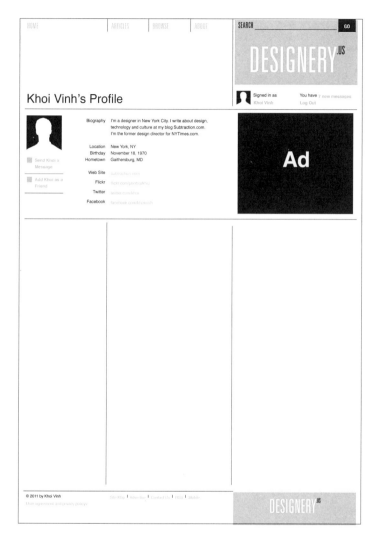

To do this we have to consider the space we're working with. We don't have room to make these thumbnails as large as similar thumbnails on the category page. However, we can reuse the dimension of the thumbnails from a similar display of projects we created on the article page design. From that page, the thumbnails were three units wide, or 170 pixels, each. Using that specification, we have the room within this six-unit, 350-pixel-wide column to fit two smaller stacks of these thumbnails side by side. The result is a presentation that's reminiscent of the category page, but more appropriate for the elements at hand.

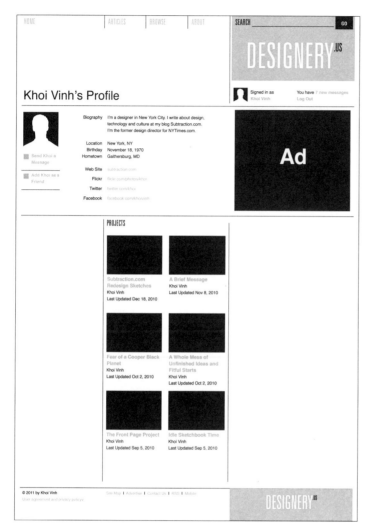

*A slightly different
presentation of
project thumbnails.*

In a slightly different vein, we'll need to reinvent the display of the user's friends, which in theory should be similar to the Top Designery users area of the category page. Recall that on that page we created a grid display of avatar icons that reveal information about the users they represent only when a user clicks.

We could recreate that presentation here, but it would be problematic. For one, we have a narrower width that is not height-limited in the way that the category page was. On that page, the grid of thumbnails had a fixed number of rows; because the network is composed of innumerable users, we only had to create a display that gave a sampling of some of those users. Here on the profile page, we're obligated to create something a bit more definitive, and that will list each avatar's true name more explicitly. So rather than trying to adapt the display from the category page, we'll create a new, more straightforward presentation here with the avatars left-aligned and users' names next to them. This also heads off another problem: this presentation is fairly lightweight and allows the column next to it to continue to carry the bulk of the page's visual weight, thereby preserving the sense of approximated symmetry.

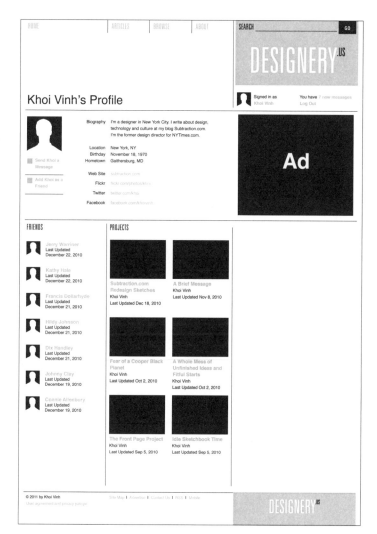

Placing the activity content in the right column.

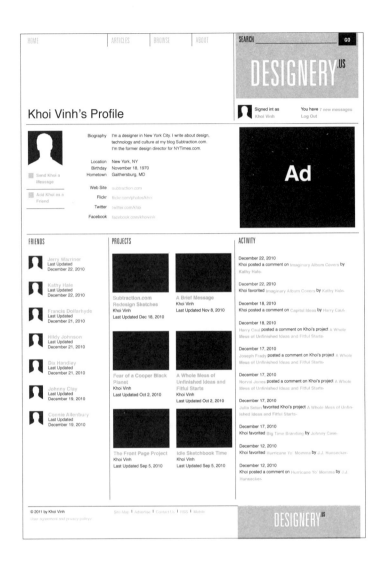

This leaves only the activity content in the right-hand column. The content itself is very straightforward—just a stream of text posts—and there's no need to complicate it. We can run the text from top to bottom in a simple column. Often, this simple approach to content works best in the far-right column anyway, as users have come to regard that region of many web pages as being full of ads. A counterintuitive approach turns out to be more effective in this area: the plainer the content, the less it looks like advertising, and therefore the more users are likely to pay attention to it.

PROJECT 4: HOME PAGE

Our last major template is the home page. Recall that we went against common practice by designing our other templates first in order to establish conventions and patterns that we can draw upon when tackling the unique challenges of the home page. As with any of our designs, we're free to adapt and make changes where necessary, but we also want to maintain consistency.

As is typical with many home pages, ours needs to serve several purposes at once: it must present a sampling of the latest and/or most interesting editorial content, it must preview some of the activity and content happening within the Designery.us social network, and it must showcase of some of the most active users of the network. What's more, it has to introduce the Designery.us brand in a way that other pages do not. The wireframe reflects these competing interests in that it's the least suggestive of a particular layout approach; in some ways, it's the most open-ended of all of them.

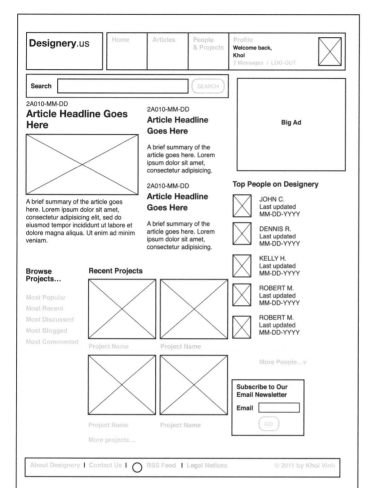

Our sketching is therefore even more critical in translating the requirements of the wireframe. We can run through several different layout ideas for this content quickly and without investing undue time and effort.

Its unique requirements make sketching even more critical for the home page.

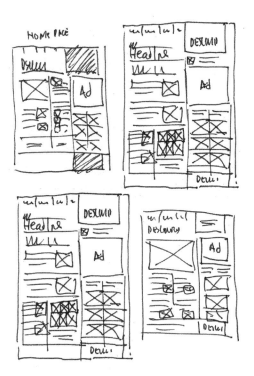

The sketch on which we'll base our design uses a fairly standard approach to arranging editorial content within a web page. It divides the page into a three main columns: a large column at far-left for the most important content, a narrower column in the middle for peripheral content, and our familiar far-right column that's carved out by the advertising unit just below the branding area.

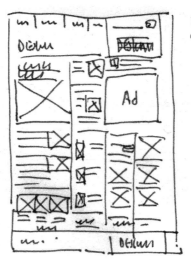

The final sketch for our home page design.

Let's start at the top of the page, where we have a unique branding requirement that we didn't encounter on other pages. As the official gateway for the site, the home page must introduce—and briefly explain—the Designery.us brand to newcomers. This could be done simply enough by including a short tagline near the branding area:

Designery is a public square for design practitioners, students, and fans.

But the right-hand positioning of the logo that we used on other pages makes it difficult to do this; such a tagline would have to be placed to the *left* of our standard branding area. That would create a kind of semantic jumble in which the explanation would appear before the concept, so to speak; what we want is the concept first and the explanation second.

To that end, we'll shift the logo out of that box and to the left, letting it stand (more or less) alone below the navigation, and we'll place the tagline in the box at right. This kind of exception makes sense for the home page because, again, it has distinct expectations. We want the brand to broadcast itself more loudly on this page, and presenting it in a manner that is unique from every other page within the site actually elevates this page in importance.

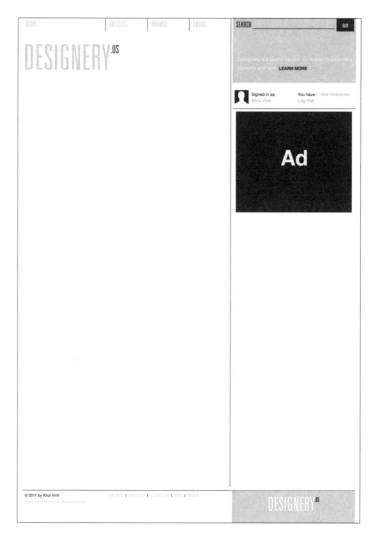

Altering the branding for the home page.

We can even help emphasize this distinction by enlarging the size of the logo. The area where it now resides has been left largely untouched on our other pages, so if we're going to make use of it here, we want to use it to maximum effect. We'll make the logo considerably larger to activate the full region, but not so large that it's uncomfortable in that area. We'll also add some bits of salutary text: a welcome statement and the date.

With the logo enlarged, the tagline has shifted further up to top-align with the logo itself. This helps the user's eye read from left-to-right, logo-to-tagline, concept-to-explanation.

Enlarging the logo activates the region.

The baseline shows how the logo and the tagline are top-aligned.

Now let's address the body of the page. Our sketch calls for three columns. We know already that the grid can support at least two different configurations of three columns: the symmetrical arrangement we created for the category page, and the configuration we created for the profile page which was more varied. In this case, a symmetrical arrangement again proves impractical because of the big ad that's required on the right-hand side, so we can turn to the three-column structure from the profile page. However, we'll transpose two of the columns so the first column is wider and calls more attention to itself. This will aid the readability of the page: in content-rich sites, the most important content usually appears at the top left of the body area—and is also usually the largest of all the content elements on the page.

The basic three-column structure we'll use for the home page.

We can follow this thinking as we design the formatting for editorial promos in these columns. As the most important article, the promo at the top of the left column will be the largest, with an accompanying image that spans the full width of the column. We can then design a secondary level of editorial promos that uses a two-unit-wide thumbnail image.

In fact, we can use this secondary promo style in the second column as well, employing the same typographic and thumbnail specifications but simply adapting the layout to the narrower width. The effect is that there is both consistency and variety in the display of these editorial elements; the eye is encouraged to scan the page for bits of interest, but the consistency within the design makes the variety easy to consume and minimizes any sense of disorder.

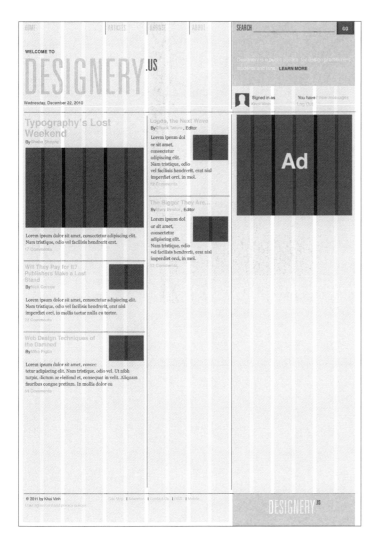

Adding article promos to the first two columns.

We can think of these five promos as presenting the most recently published content on Designery.us, but each is large enough to require a fairly healthy share of screen real estate, so a more space-efficient promo style could come in handy as well. At the bottom of the first column, we can create a third level of editorial promos that omits summaries and therefore takes up less space. These promos will use the same two-unit thumbnails we've employed in the secondary-level promos, but we'll arrange them three across.

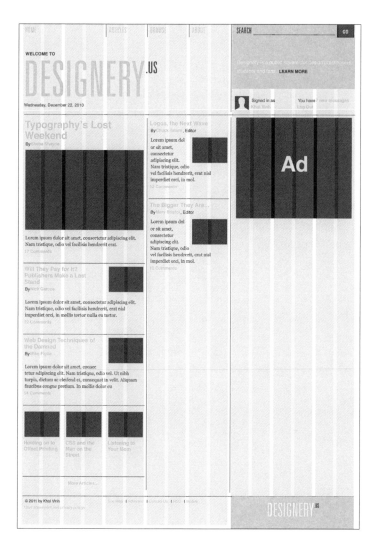

Because they're succinct, the placement of these promos at the bottom of the column has a useful logic to it; they suggest that there is more of this kind of content available throughout the site. And in fact we can reinforce that by adding a "More Articles..." link at the bottom of the column.

Our wireframe now calls for several elements that should be familiar from other templates. In the middle column, we can duplicate our email subscription form from the article page as well as the list of users from the profile page.

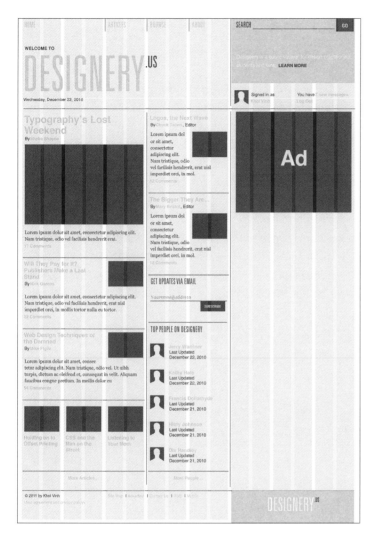

Elements familiar from other pages, like the email subscription form and a list of people and avatar icons, are easily placed in the middle column.

In the far-right column, we can borrow the display of projects we created for the profile page. This column is also six units wide, so that element fits in nicely.

The wireframe also calls for a list of links to help users find the projects that are most popular, most discussed, most recently updated, and so forth. We'll want these to appear above the projects so users can find them easily (rather than below the projects, which would be too far down the page). Looking again to the category page, we designed links similar to these that appeared within a column that was narrower than the six-unit column we have here. Though we actually have more width than we did on the category page, here we have less height for the vertical display of these links, so we can divide the list into two narrower sub-columns of three links each, with less generous line-spacing than we used before.

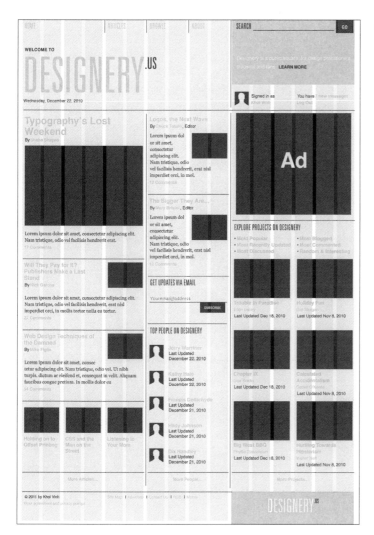

Adding projects to
the far-right column.

Like the editorial articles, the lists of users and projects are intended to lead users to more of the same content. Again, this is the purpose of the home page: to show a sampling of what's available on Designery.us. So we can use the convention we created for the "More Articles..." link for both users and projects at the bottom of the second and third columns. This suggests that the page has a simple ordering principle: articles in the left column, users in the middle, and projects on the right. Though that's actually not exactly true—we're mixing content within columns more freely than that—it's true enough in that it *appears* orderly. In many cases, that's plenty.

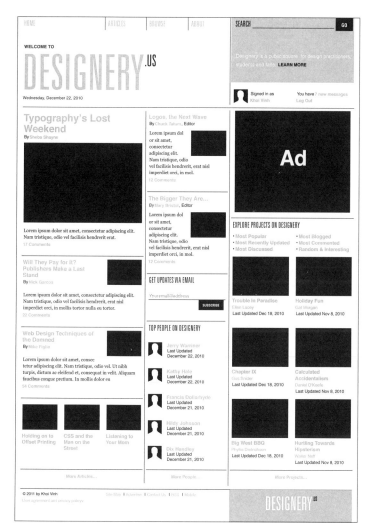

The final home page design.

ADDITIONAL PAGES

The four templates we've created so far—article page, category page, profile page, and home page—offer four distinctly different layout approaches within our grid system. These are also the pages that users will probably encounter most often, and so in many ways they provide a substantially diverse base on which to build out the rest of the site.

However, in a site rich with content and interactions, we want to be mindful not to blindly recycle layout conventions when other pages on the site pose different constraints and therefore call for different approaches. Our job is not simply to design on a page-by-page basis without regard for the overall combination of pages a user might encounter. Even though it's impossible to know the exact sequence any particular user might follow while browsing Designery.us, we can anticipate some models. A user might move from home page to article to article and perhaps back to the home page, for instance, or move from category page to profile page to other templates we have not yet designed, such as project pages.

In acknowledging this reality, we understand that the *sequencing* of our designs is part of our job. As the user moves from page to page, our goal is to help him acquire a kind of spatial understanding of the parts of the site, so that the various interfaces oriented around social networking resemble one another and the kinds of editorial content are similar. At the highest level, however, we must do our best to ensure that the layouts he encounters are consistent where appropriate and divergent where appropriate. Here are some examples of how we might use the groundwork we've already laid to create a diverse and surprising but easily navigable and consistent experience.

AUTHOR PAGE

An author page is conceptually similar to our profile page, and it would be tempting to base its design on that existing template. However, the kind of content offered on this page is actually closer to our article template; it's editorially focused, not social network–focused. So it makes more sense to create a design that is principally based on the layout we created for the article template.

ABOUT US PAGE

We can take the same approach to designing the about us page, which offers the site's mission statement, history, and short biographies of its founders. Again, we'll borrow the article template's two-thirds/one-third layout. This page will be a bit more spare, though, so we'll omit the vertical dividing rule that demarcates the two main content areas from biographies of the founders in the right-column.

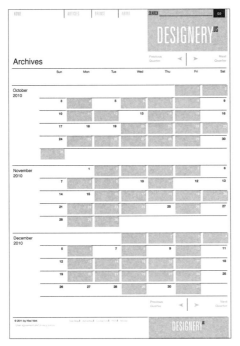

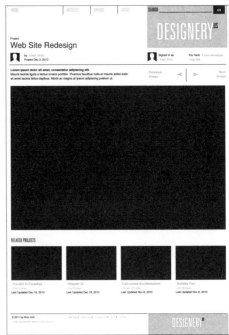

ARCHIVES PAGE

Not every editorially focused template needs
to follow the same model as the article page.
We can imagine that a date-based archive
page would follow an entirely different
approach. It would use the calendar as its
central metaphor for organization—and as
its central metaphor for layout.

PROJECT PAGE

The projects featured on the Designery.us
templates we've created so far must go
somewhere, and that destination is the
project page. In actuality, it's nothing more
than a simple, slideshow-style interface that
allows users to peruse the various images
within a project.

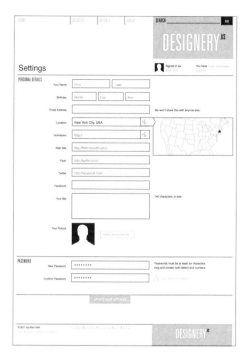

SETTINGS PAGE

Settings pages are often complex, but we can use the grid to help simplify their presentation. For the Designery.us settings pages, the various details are arranged in a six-unit column with labels for each element hanging to the left in a four-unit column.

EMAIL TEMPLATE

Finally, it's worth noting that our grid doesn't have to be confined to the site. We can also export it to other media. For example, the Designery.us email newsletter that users subscribe to can still benefit from the work we've done on the site.

LIQUID LAYOUTS

The layout templates we've created have all been based on the idea that they will have a fixed width; that is, the width of units, columns, regions, and so on will remain constant even in cases where the user might expand his browser window to a much greater size than the design itself. In fact, most commercially viable websites have followed this pattern for the better part of the Web's existence. It has proven to be the most effective and successful layout technique for bringing thoughtful design values to a medium that isn't always conducive to such things.

However, I would be remiss if I didn't discuss the alternative notion of *liquid layouts*, or layouts that expand and contract with the user's viewport.

If, as designers, we are charged with creating experiences that truly respect our users' preferences, there is a valid argument *against* fixed-width layouts and *for* liquid layouts. In effect, a fixed-width layout reflects the imposition of the designer's penchant for control over real-world usage, while designs that grow in width or even in height to accommodate the user's viewport can be said to truly reflect each user's requirements.

For users with large monitors, you could argue, a design should expand to capitalize on the available real estate, while for users with smaller monitors or devices, the design should condense appropriately. It might not be quite accurate to say that liquid layouts attempt to be all things to all users, but the aim is similar. The Web is a medium in which systems try to serve broad swaths of people in ways that are most appropriate to each of their needs. But no two people will experience a given website's content or functionality in exactly the same way, so why should the same layout apply to all of them? In many ways, liquid layouts really are more native to the medium—more faithful to its strengths and weakness—than fixed-width layouts. And, as we discussed earlier in this book, the more native the solution, the more effective it's likely to be.

Until very recently, the state of Web design didn't allow us to live up to the ideal presented by liquid layouts. Advancements in browser capabilities, coupled with innovations in CSS and newly reliable JavaScript techniques for creating experiences that are more thoroughly device-aware, have begun to allow designers to create much more dynamic layouts.

Ambitious designers can now practice so-called "responsive Web design," which, according to prominent proponent Ethan Marcotte, opens up new possibilities:

"We can design for an optimal viewing experience, but embed standards-based technologies into our designs to make them not only more flexible, but more adaptive to the media that renders them."

These breakthroughs are incredibly new and evolving rapidly, which is why I have chosen not to address them in this book. Best practices are still being written in the realm of responsive Web design.

However, some basic design principles will stand regardless of how this new approach develops. In particular, it will remain true that while designers must continue to share control over the experiences of their products with users, those users want *guided experiences*. It's a mistake to assume that responsive Web design means giving users full control, because in reality what every user wants is only *some control*. Users expect the designer not only to have embraced the medium, but also to have mastered it sufficiently to be able to exert some control over it.

It will always remain the designer's job to make some decisions for the user—not every decision, but enough to provide guideposts within the experience that the user can turn to. The designer must empower the user to feel in control of the aspects of the experience that are critical to accomplishing his goals, but the user must also feel that the entire experience has an underpinning of stability and reliability.

Responsive Web design doesn't make that job simpler. In fact, it makes it more complex. There will be even more states for the designer to anticipate, more combinations of user interface elements in varying states presenting unique but critical challenges to the user's understanding of the experience. In this respect, the grid will become even more important to the overall design; establishing a strong grid system that underpins a responsive Web design solution can only help it feel more rooted and trustworthy.

The same basic grid principles can apply in this world of liquid layouts and responsive Web design. Units can be combined into columns and regions, and elements can be sized according to the basic mathematics of the grid. Those elements should grow and condense according to those same mathematics, but it's important to remember that not everything needs to change. Some things can remain fixed; in fact, some things must remain fixed. In an environment where elements can assume an endless combination of sizes and scales, it's even more important to maintain some constancy, to establish some guideposts to help orient users. As this school of thought continues to gain momentum, it promises to create great opportunities for designers working in this medium. At the same time, it doesn't change the designer's central role as the arbiter of the user's experience.

Chapter 5
Conclusion

As I close out this tour of my approach to grid-based design for the Web, I thought it appropriate to note the trajectory of Web design over its short history.

The typographic grid that informed countless posters, books, magazines, and other highly expressive forms of design authorship is still something of a novelty in digital media. With time, as tools and technologies change and as more design writers and thinkers interpret the fundamentals of the grid for new technological frontiers, grids may become more pervasive and more integral to the presentation of digital content and features. And certainly, with the continual improvements in the technology that renders the experiences that we interface with, grids can play a more important—and useful—role in digital media in the coming years.

This book seeks to aid in that transition, to propagate grid principles in the hope that they can influence how design is practiced on the World Wide Web and indeed in all digital media—for the better. However, don't make the mistake of thinking that this book anticipates a future where the Web or any other digital platform will resemble the world of print and analog media any more than it does today. Just the opposite is true, in fact.

As technology pushes forward, our word-based media will continue to look less and less like what came before. Technical innovations will shape and reshape our interactions. More importantly, user behaviors will continue to evolve, spurring new modes of interaction within our platforms. All of this will continue to present new opportunities and challenges for designers. And as design problems change, so will design solutions.

Developing design solutions based on grids is not a way to recreate the glory of an older medium within the framework of the new one. In fact, for grid principles to effect a truly positive change on the Web or in any digital medium, the designer must adapt and change them to suit the problems she faces. There are many lessons to be learned from how grids have been developed in the past, and there are many rules to master in their usage today. But the most important idea of all is that the designer must deeply understand the problem she's trying to solve and create a truly appropriate solution for it.

Appendix

No book on grids will suffice in and of itself for the truly ambitious designer. As with design in general, the more you feed your knowledge and skills with the learned wisdom or new thinking of other practitioners, the greater your personal growth as a designer. To that end, here is a selection of the best reading on grids, design, and code that I've encountered. It's an incomplete list—any one of these books or links will lead you to countless other sources of inspiration. I encourage you to follow those trails as far as they'll take you.

A final note: in addition to these resources, you'll find late additions to this list, supplemental notes and much more at the companion site to this book: **http://grids.subtraction.com**

GRIDS

- *The Typographic Grid* by Hans Rudolf Bosshard
- *A Practical Guide to Designing Grid Systems for the Web* by Mark Boulton
- *Grid Systems: Principles of Organizing Type* by Kimberly Elam
- *Geometry of Design* by Kimberly Elam
- *The Grid Book* by Hannah B. Higgins
- *The Grid* by Allen Hurlburt
- *Grid Systems in Graphic Design* by Josef Müller-Brockmann
- *The Designer and the Grid* by Lucienne Roberts and Julia Thrift
- *Making and Breaking the Grid* by Timothy Samara

ONLINE GRID RESOURCES

- The Grid System — http://www.thegridsystem.org
- Five Simple Steps to Designing Grid Systems by Mark Boulton — http://bit.ly/atBRYh
- Grid Based Designs — http://grid-based.com
- Gridness — http://gridness.net
- Blueprint CSS Framework — http://www.blueprintcss.org
- 960 Grid System — http://960.gs
- Responsive Web Design — http://responsivewebdesign.com/
- Fluidgrid — http://fluid.newgoldleaf.com/

DESIGNERS

- *Unimark International* by Jan Conradi
- *Paul Rand* by Steven Heller
- *Swiss Graphic Design: The Origins and Growth of an International Style, 1920-1965* by Richard Hollis
- *Corporate Diversity: Swiss Graphic Design and Advertising by Geigy, 1940-1970,* Museum für Gestaltung Zürich
- *Josef Müller-Brockmann: Pioneer of Swiss Graphic Design* by Lars Muller and Paul Rand
- *Josef Müller-Brockmann* by Kerry William Purcell
- *Otl Aicher* by Markus Rathgeb
- *Design Is One* by Lella and Massimo Vignelli

TYPOGRAPHY

- *The Elements of Typographic Style* by Robert Bringhurst
- *TypeWise* by Kit Hinrichs
- *Thinking with Type: A Critical Guide for Designers, Writers, Editors, & Students* by Ellen Lupton
- *Stop Stealing Sheep & Find Out How Type Works* by Erik Spiekermann
- *The New Typography* by Jan Tschichold and E.M. Ginger

HTML AND CSS

- *Bulletproof Web Design* by Dan Cederholm
- *Web Standards Solutions: The Markup and Style Handbook* by Dan Cederholm
- *Eric Meyer on CSS* by Eric Meyer
- *Designing with Web Standards* by Jeffrey Zeldman with Ethan Marcotte

INTERACTION DESIGN AND THINKING

- *About Face 3: The Essentials of Interaction Design* by Alan Cooper
- *The Inmates Are Running the Asylum: Why Tech Products Drive Us Crazy and How to Restore the Sanity* by Alan Cooper, Robert Reimann, and David Cronin
- *Don't Make Me Think: A Common Sense Approach to Web Usability* by Steve Krug
- *Designing Web Usability* by Jakob Nielsen
- *Designing for Interaction: Creating Innovative Applications and Devices* by Dan Saffer
- *Designing Interfaces: Patterns for Effective Interaction Design* by Jennifer Tidwell
- *Glut: Mastering Information Through the Ages* by Alex Wright

Index